NATIONAL DIRECTORY
OF
LOW-COST TOURIST
ATTRACTIONS

NATIONAL DIRECTORY
OF
LOW-COST TOURIST
ATTRACTIONS

Edited by

RAYMOND CARLSON

PILOT BOOKS • NEW YORK

Library of Congress Catalog Card Number: 79-12044

Library of Congress Cataloging in Publication Data

Carlson, Raymond.
    National directory of low cost tourist attractions.

    1.   United States—Description and travel—1960-
—Guide-books.   2.   Historic sites—United States—
Guide-books.   I.   Title.
E158.C32   917.3′04′926   79-12044
ISBN 0-87576-080-5

Printed in United States of America

CONTENTS

WHY THIS BOOK WAS WRITTEN

This first edition of the NATIONAL DIRECTORY OF LOW-COST TOURIST ATTRACTIONS offers you a state by state, geographical listing of a wide range of attractions for family enjoyment. More than 900 locations are listed with brief descriptions.

This directory shows you where to find castles, battleships, prehistoric caves, pioneer forts, boom towns, Southern plantations, restored villages, space capsules, zoos, famous museums, even a mule cemetery. You can also locate many of our national parks, battlefields, monuments, cemeteries, historical sites, natural and man-made wonders, and other low-cost tourist attractions.

A low-cost tourist attraction is defined as one that charges an adult admission fee that is less than $2.50. For children the entrance fee is generally half the adult price. Infants are normally admitted free. Many attractions also offer senior citizen discounts. All attractions that are free for kids, cost under $1, or have an admission by donation policy are so indicated in the listings. Children are usually admitted free only if accompanied by an adult. Admission days and hours have also been included. However, since many attractions change their admission policy so frequently, it's always a good idea to phone or write the site of your choice before going.

Another good tip is to bring along your picnic basket. Many attractions provide picnic areas. This information is also included in the listings.

Every effort has been made to compile an accurate, up-to-date directory, but changes do occur. Your editor welcomes new information on any of the listings.

So whether your family leans toward prehistoric ruins or popcorn at the zoo, crowds or quiet, you'll no doubt find it in this directory.

Have fun!

NATIONAL DIRECTORY OF LOW-COST TOURIST ATTRACTIONS

(All low-cost tourist attractions are listed without charge. While the entries are believed to be from reliable sources, the author and publisher do not vouch for or guarantee them, nor is responsibility assumed for transactions which may result from publishing this type of information.)

ALABAMA

BIRMINGHAM
ARLINGTON ANTEBELLUM HOME & GARDENS (19th-century estate, antiques, self-guided tours), 331 Cotton Ave., S.W., Daily 9:00 - 5:00, Sunday 1:00 - 6:00, 205-780-5656, Kids (under 6) free
BIRMINGHAM ZOO (over 1,000 animals, birds & reptiles, picnicking), 2630 Cahaba Rd., Daily 9:30 - 5:00, 205-879-0408, Kids under $1
OAK MOUNTAIN STATE PARK DEMONSTRATION FARM (visitor center, swimming, picnicking), US 31 S., Daily 10:00 - 6:00, 205-663-6771, Under $1

CULLMAN
AVE MARIA GROTTO (Benedictine monk's lifetime creation, over 150 miniature religious structures, settings & shrines constructed from scraps), US 31, Daily 7:00 - sunset, Kids under $1

FLORENCE
W.C. HANDY HOUSE (historic log cabin, period furnishings, memorabilia, museum), 620 West College St., Daily 9:00 - 4:00 (closed Monday & Sunday), 205-766-2662, Kids under $1
INDIAN MOUND MUSEUM (largest prehistoric mound on the Tennessee River), South Court St., Daily 9:00 - 4:00 (closed Monday & Sunday), 205-766-2662, Kids under $1
POPE'S TAVERN (early 19th-century house, from stage stop & tavern to Confederate hospital), 203 Hermitage Dr., Daily 9:00 - 4:00 (closed Monday & Sunday), 205-766-2662, Kids under $1

GADSDEN
NOCCALULA FALLS PARK PIONEER MUSEUM (homestead, botanical gardens, picnicking), I-59 (Exit 188) US 431, Daily 9:00 - sunset, 205-543-9870, Kids under $1

MOBILE
JASMINE HILL GARDEN (12 acres of Greek sculpture, art objects, fountains, pools), US 231, Summer: Daily 9:00 - 5:00 (closed Monday), 205-263-1440, Kids under $1
MONTGOMERY ZOO (animals, birds, reptiles, picnicking), 329 Vandiver, Summer: Daily 9:30 - 6:00, 205-265-3536, Under $1
OAKLEIGH MANSION (historic house museum, period furnishings, regional items, garden), 350 Oakleigh Place, Daily 10:00 - 4:00, Sunday 2:00 - 4:00, 205-431-1281, Kids (under 12) free
ORDEMAN-SHAW HISTORICAL HOME (mid 19th-century restored home, period items, museum, gardens), 220 N. Hull St., Daily 9:30 - 4:00, Sunday 1:30 - 4:00, 205-265-4149, Kids (under 6) free

W.A. GAYLE PLANETARIUM (changing shows), 1010 Forest Ave., Daily 9:00 - 5:00, Weekends 1:00 - 5:00, 205-265-6225, Kids under $1

MOUNDVILLE (Tuscaloosa)
MOUND STATE MONUMENT (restored Indian village, archaeological museum, burial ground, picnicking), Rt. 69, Daily 9:00 - 5:00, 205-371-2572

SELMA
STURDIVANT HALL (19th-century restored mansion, slave quarters, gardens, tours), 713 Mabry St., Daily 9:00 - 4:00, Sunday 2:00 - 4:00 (closed Monday), Kids (under 12) free

TUSCALOOSA
STRICKLAND HOUSE (mid 19th-century historic house, period items), 6th Street, Daily 9:00 - 5:00 (closed Weekends), By donation

TUSCUMBIA
IVY GREEN (Helen Keller's birthplace, family furniture, memorabilia), 300 W. North Commons, Daily 8:30 - 4:30, Sunday 1:00 - 4:30, 205-383-4066, Kids (under 6) free

WARRIOR (Birmingham)
RICHWOOD CAVERNS & STATE PARK (cave tours, picnicking), I-65, US 31, Richwood Caverns Rd., Daily 10:00 - 6:00, 205-647-9692

ALASKA

ANCHORAGE
ALASKA ZOO (children's petting area), O'Malley Rd., Summer: Daily, 907-344-8012
ANCHORAGE HISTORICAL & FINE ARTS MUSEUM (Alaskan artifacts, art, history, science, tours), 121 West 7th Ave., Summer: Daily 9:00 - 5:00, Sunday 1:00 - 5:00, 907-279-1553

FAIRBANKS
UNIVERSITY OF ALASKA MUSEUM (natural history, Eskimo artifacts, tours), University of Alaska, Summer: Daily 9:00 - 5:00, 907-479-7505
ALASKALAND (theme park, museum, picnicking), 901 First Ave., Summer: Daily, 907-452-4244

JUNEAU
ALASKA STATE MUSEUM (natural history museum, Alaskan artifacts, early industry, tours), Subport, Pouch F.M., Summer: Daily 9:00 - 4:00, Weekends 1:00 - 9:00, 907-586-1224

KETCHIKAN
TONGASS HISTORICAL SOCIETY MUSEUM (Alaskan Indian artifacts, anthropology, archaeology tours), 629 Dock St., Summer: Daily 11:00 - 5:00, Weekends 1:00 - 4:00, 907-225-5600

KODIAK
OLD RUSSIAN WAREHOUSE (late 18th-century structure, oldest Russian building in country, regional artifacts, folklore, tours), Kodiak Historical Society, 101 Marine Way, Summer: Daily 11:00 - 3:00, Weekends 1:00 - 4:00, 907-486-5920, By donation

SITKA
SHELDON JACKSON MUSEUM (Eskimo artifacts, totem poles, Russian orthodox religious items, tours), Sheldon Jackson College, Summer: Daily 8:00 - 5:00, 907-747-5228

ARIZONA

CAMP VERDE
MONTEZUMA CASTLE NATIONAL MONUMENT (one of the best preserved cliff dwellings in the U.S., visitor center, limited picnicking), I-17, Summer: Daily 7:00 - 7:00, 602-567-3322, Vehicle use fee charged

CLARKDALE
TUZIGOOT NATIONAL MONUMENT (excavated ruins of a large prehistoric pueblo, self-guiding trails, visitor center), US 89 ALT., Rt. 279, Summer: Daily 7:00 - 7:00, 602-634-5564, Vehicle use fee charged

COOLIDGE
CASA GRANDE RUINS NATIONAL MONUMENT (Indian ruins, museum, tours, picnicking), Rt. 87, Daily 7:00 - 6:00, 602-723-3172, Vehicle use fee charged

FLAGSTAFF
WALNUT CANYON NATIONAL MONUMENT (over 300 prehistoric cliff dwellings, visitor center, self-guided trails, picnicking), I-40, US 66, Summer: Daily 7:00 - 7:00, 602-526-3367, Vehicle use fee charged

GANADO
HUBBELL TRADING POST NATIONAL HISTORIC SITE (living history area, museum, tours), Rt. 264 W., Daily 8:00 - 5:00, 602-755-3475, Under $1

GRAND CANYON
GRAND CANYON NATIONAL PARK (one of the world's most spectacular natural wonders, visitor center, museum, self-guided trails, picnicking), Rt. 64, Summer: Daily (south-rim) 7:00 - 9:00 P.M., 602-638-2411, Vehicle use fee charged

HOLBROOK
PETRIFIED FOREST NATIONAL PARK (world's largest natural exhibit of petrified wood, Indian ruins, visitor center, picnicking), US 180, Summer: Daily 7:00 - sunset, Vehicle use fee charged

NOGALES
TUMACACORI NATIONAL MONUMENT (historic Spanish Catholic mission, museum, patio garden, picnicking) US 89, Daily 8:00 - 5:00, 602-398-2341, Vehicle use fee charged

PHOENIX
ARIZONA MUSEUM (Indian collection, pioneer artifacts), 1002 W. Van Buren St., Summer: Daily 2:00 - 5:00 (closed Monday & Tuesday), 602-253-2734, By donation
DESERT BOTANICAL GARDEN (over 150 acres of desert plants, museum, tours), Papago Park, 5800 E. Van Buren St., Daily 9:00 - 5:00, 602-947-2800, Kids under $1
HALL OF FLAME (early firefighting equipment), 110 N. Project Dr., Daily 9:00 - 5:00, 602-275-3473, Kids under $1
HEARD MUSEUM (anthropology & primitive art collection), 22 E. Monte Vista Rd., Daily 10:00 - 5:00, Sunday 1:00 - 5:00, 602-252-8848
PHOENIX ZOO (over 1,000 animals & birds, picnicking), Papago Park, US 60, 80, 89, Summer: Daily 9:00 - 7:00, 602-273-1341, Kids under $1
TROPIC GARDEN ZOO (kiddie petting area & rides), 6232 N. 7th St., Daily 9:00 - 5:00, 602-279-9707, Kids (under 11) less than $1

ROOSEVELT
TONTO NATIONAL MONUMENT (well-preserved cliff dwellings, guided tours, visitor center, picnicking), Rt. 88, Daily 8:00 - 5:00, 602-467-2241, Vehicle use fee charged

TOMBSTONE
BOOTHILL GRAVEYARD (burial grounds for Old-West characters), US 80 N., Daily 8:00 - 6:00, 602-457-3972, By donation
O.K. CORRAL (scene of the Early-West gunfight), Allen St. (between 3rd & 4th), Daily 9:00 - 5:00, 602-457-2227, Kids under $1
SCHIEFFELIN HALL'S TOMBSTONE HISTORAMA (old Tombstone's history, electronic diorama), 4th & Fremont, Daily: shows begin at 9:30, last show 3:30, 602-457-2227, Kids under $1
TOMBSTONE COURTHOUSE HISTORICAL PARK (regional & pioneer artifacts), US 80, Daily 8:00 - 5:30, 602-457-3311, Under $1
WELLS FARGO MUSEUM (Old-West items, wax figures of legendary characters), 511 Allen St., Daily 9:00 - 5:00, 602-457-2254, Kids under $1

TUCSON
COLOSSAL CAVE (guided tours, picnicking), I-10 (Exit 279 N.) Colossal Cave Rd. (Vail), Daily 8:00 - 6:00, Sunday & Holidays 8:00 - 7:00, 602-791-7677, Kids (under 6) free
RANDOLPH PARK CHILDREN'S ZOO (picnicking), B'way (near 22nd), Daily 9:30 - 5:00, 602-791-4475, Under $1
SAGUARO NATIONAL MONUMENT/RINCON MT. SECTION (cactus forest, self-auto tours, visitor center, picnicking), US 10, E. B'way, Daily 8:00 - 5:00, 602-298-2036, Vehicle use fee charged

WILLCOX
CHIRICAHUA NATIONAL MONUMENT (wilderness of unusual rock shapes, museum, picnicking), Rt. 186, Daily 8:00 - 5:00, 602-824-3560, Under $1

WINSLOW
GREAT METEOR CRATER (the diameter of the rim measures over 4,000 feet, museum, lectures), I-40, Great Meteor Crater Rd., Summer: Daily 7:00 - sunset, Kids (under 8) free

ARKANSAS

BERRYVILLE
COSMIC CAVERNS (tours, picnicking), Rt. 21, Summer: Daily 8:00 - 7:00, 501-749-2298
SAUNDERS MUSEUM (handgun collection, antiques, regional items), Rt. 21, Daily 9:00 - 5:00 (closed Nov. through Mar. 14), 501-423-2563, Kids under $1

EUREKA SPRINGS
BLUE SPRINGS ATTRACTIONS (one of the Ozark's largest springs, multimedia shows), US 62, Summer: Daily 8:00 - 7:00, 501-253-9244, Kids (under 6) free
CHRIST ONLY ART GALLERY (over 350 works of art featuring Jesus), US 62, Summer: Daily 8:00 - 8:00, 501-253-8211, Kids under $1
HOLIDAY ISLAND ANIMAL PARK (sea shows, petting zoo, picnicking), US 62, Summer: Daily 9:00 - 5:00, 501-253-9696
ONYX CAVE PARK (cave tours, Gay 90's museum, picnicking), US 62, Summer: Daily 8:00 - 8:00, 501-253-9321, Kids (under 6) free

ROSALIE HISTORIC HOUSE (turn-of-the-century home, museum, original furnishings), 282 Spring St., Summer: Daily 9:30 - 5:30, 501-253-9655, Kids under $1

HOT SPRINGS
ARKANSAS ALLIGATOR FARM (zoo, alligators, snakes, monkeys), 847 Whittington Ave., Summer: Daily 8:00 - 5:00, 501-623-6171, Kids under $1
I. Q. ZOO (animal shows, zoo, tours), 380 Whittington Ave., Summer: Daily 9:00 - 5:00, 501-623-7572, Kids under $1

LITTLE ROCK
ARKANSAS TERRITORIAL RESTORATION (13 authentic 1880's buildings, period furnishings, guided tours), 214 E. 3rd St., Daily 9:00 - 5:00, Sunday 1:00 - 5:00, 501-371-2348, Kids under $1

MORRILTON
MUSEUM OF AUTOMOBILES (horseless carriages, classic chrome), I-40 (Exit Morrilton), Daily 10:00 - 5:00, 501-727-5427, Kids (under 6) free

MOUNTAIN VIEW
OZARK FOLK CENTER (native craftsmen, woodcarving, quiltmaking, live musical entertainment, petting zoo, picnicking), Rt. 382, Summer: Daily 9:00 - 6:00, Kids (under 6) free

MURFREESBORO
CRATER OF DIAMONDS STATE PARK (search for diamonds, museum, picnicking), Rt. 301, Daily 8:00 - 5:00, 501-285-3113, Kids (under 6) free

ROGERS
PEA RIDGE NATIONAL MILITARY PARK (major Civil War battle scene, visitor center, self-auto tour, picnicking), US 62, Summer: Daily 8:00 - 6:00, 501-451-8122, Vehicle use fee charged

CALIFORNIA

ATASCADERO
ATASCADERO PARK ZOO (picnicking), Rt. 41, Summer: Daily 10:00 - 5:00, 805-466-9037, By donation

BARSTOW
CALICO GHOST TOWN (restored Old-West mining town, museum, railroad, picnicking), I-15 to Ghost Town Rd., Summer: Daily 8:00 - 6:00, 714-254-2122, Parking fee charged

BURBANK
NBC T.V. STUDIO TOURS (guided tours), 3000 W. Alameda Ave., Monday - Saturday 10:00 - 5:00, 213-845-7000

FT. BRAGG
MENDOCINO COAST BOTANICAL GARDENS (over 45 acres, guided tours, trails, streams, picnicking), Rt. 1, Summer: Daily 8:30 - 6:00, 707-964-4352, Kids (under 6) free

FRESNO
ROEDING PARK ZOO & CHILDREN'S STORYLAND (over 700 animals & birds, petting & feeding area, gardens, picnicking), 894 W. Belmont Ave., Summer: Daily 10:00 - 5:00, 209-488-3033, Under $1

KLAMATH
TREES OF MYSTERY (redwood forest, tree carvings, Indian museum), US 101, Daily 7:00 - sunset, 707-482-5613

LOMPOC
LA PURISIMA MISSION STATE PARK (restored 1787 mission, history museum, picnicking), Rt. 1 to Casmalia Rd., Daily 9:00 - 5:00, 805-733-3713, Kids free

LOS ANGELES
GRIFFITH OBSERVATORY & PLANETARIUM (twin refracting telescope, planetarium shows, museum, picnicking), Griffith Park, 2800 E. Observatory Rd., Observatory: Daily 2:00 - 10:00, Saturday 10:30 - 1:00, Sunday 1:00 - 10:00, Check for planetarium shows, 213-664-1181, Observatory free
LOS ANGELES ZOO (includes children's zoo, over 100 acres, natural exhibit areas, picnicking), Griffith Park, 5333 Zoo Dr., Summer: Daily 10:00 - 6:00, 213-661-2184, Kids (under 12) free

MARTINEZ
JOHN MUIR NATIONAL HISTORIC SITE (Muir home & adjacent Martinez Abode, visitor center, self-guiding trails, picnicking), Rt. 4, Daily 8:30 - 4:30, 415-228-8860, Kids (under 16) free

MINERAL
LASSEN VOLCANIC NATIONAL PARK (impressive volcanic phenomena, Lassen Peak, our most recently active volcano 1914 - 1921, visitor center, picnicking), Rt. 36, Daily (visitor center: Summer only 8:00 - 5:00), Vehicle use fee charged

MURPHYS
MERCER CAVERNS (cave tours, picnicking), Rt. 4, Summer: Daily 9:00 - 5:00, 209-728-2101, Kids under $1

OAKLAND
OAKLAND MUSEUM (huge art, science & history complex, galleries, gardens, exhibits), 10th & Oak St., Daily 10:00 - 5:00 (closed Monday), 415-273-3401, Under $1
OAKLAND ZOO & OAKLAND BABY ZOO (Over 300 animals & birds, Zoo-Fari sky ride, petting & feeding area, picnicking), Knowland Park, US 50, I-580, Baby Zoo: Daily 9:00 - 5:00, 415-569-4065, Kids under $1

PACIFIC PALISADES
WILL ROGERS STATE PARK (over 180 acres, the Rogers home, memorabilia, picnicking), 14253 Sunset Blvd., Summer: Daily 10:00 - 5:00, 213-454-8212

PALM DESERT
LIVING DESERT RESERVE (wildlife reserve, aquarium, gardens, trails, museum), 47-900 Portola Ave., Open Sept. through end of May 9:00 - 5:00, 714-346-5694, Kids under $1

PERRIS
ORANGE EMPIRE RAILROAD & TROLLEY MUSEUM (early trolleys, railroad items, train ride, picnicking), 2201 South "A" St., Daily 9:00 - 5:00, 714-657-2605, Free (pay for rides)

SACRAMENTO
SCIENCE CENTER & JUNIOR MUSEUM (science & natural history exhibits, films), 3615 Auburn Blvd., Daily 9:30 - 5:00, Sunday 1:00 - 5:00, 916-485-4471, Under $1
SUTTER'S FORT STATE PARK (restored Early-West outpost, antique wagons, Indian museum, tours), 28th & L St., Daily 10:00 - 5:00, 916-445-4209, Under $1

WILLIAM LAND PARK ZOO & FAIRYTALE TOWN (amusement rides, picnicking), Freeport Blvd., Daily 9:00 - 4:30, 916-447-5094, Under $1

SAN DIEGO
MARITIME MUSEUM (iron sailing ship, steam ferry & yacht, exhibits), 1306 N. Harbor Dr., Daily 9:00 - 8:00, 714-234-9153, Kids under $1
MUSEUM OF MAN (the story of early man, regional items), Balboa Park, Daily 10:00 - 4:30, 714-239-2001, Under $1
NATURAL HISTORY MUSEUM (exhibits of natural resources), Balboa Park, Daily 10:00 - 4:30, 714-232-3821, Kids (under 16) free
SAN DIEGO ZOO (one of the world's biggest zoos, thousands of wild animals & birds, children's zoo, moving sidewalks, picnicking), Balboa Park, Daily 9:00 - 5:00, 714-231-1515, Kids (under 16) free
WHALEY HOUSE (restored historical site museum, "The Old Town Drug Store," gardens), 2482 San Diego Ave., Daily 10:00 - 4:00 (closed Monday & Tuesday), 714-298-2482, Kids under $1

SAN FRANCISCO
CALIFORNIA ACADEMY OF SCIENCES (planetarium, aquarium, natural history museum), Golden Gate Park, Daily 10:00 - 5:00, 415-221-5100, Under $1
CALIFORNIA PALACE OF THE LEGION OF HONOR (18th century French art, restored rooms), Lincoln Park, Daily 10:00 - 5:00, 415-558-2881, Under $1
CHINATOWN WAX MUSEUM (over 30 historical scenes), 601 Grant Ave., Daily 10:00 - 11:00, 415-392-1011, Kids (under 6) free
MISSION DOLORES (one of San Francisco's oldest structures, pioneer cemetery), Dolores St., Summer: Daily 9:00 - 5:00, 415-621-8203, Under $1
MUIR WOODS NATIONAL MONUMENT (virgin strand of coast redwood, over 500 acres, nature trails), Rt. 1 (Mill Valley), Daily 8:00 - sunset, 415-388-2595, Under $1
SAN FRANCISCO HISTORIC SHIPS (restored sailing ships, steam vessels, tours), Aquatic Park, Hyde Street Pier, Summer: Daily 10:00 - 6:00, 415-556-6435, Kids free
SAN FRANCISCO MARITIME MUSEUM (models of old-time sailing ships, photos, marine memorabilia), Aquatic Park, foot of Polk St., Daily 10:00 - 5:00, 415-673-0700, Kids (under 12) free
SAN FRANCISCO ZOO (over 1,000 animals, birds & reptiles, children's zoo, rides, picnicking), Skyline Blvd. to Zoo Ave., Daily 10:00 - 5:00, 415-661-2023

SAN JOSE
HAPPY HOLLOW CHILDREN'S PLAYGROUND & BABY ZOO (baby animals, petting area, puppet shows, tree house, rides), Kelley Park, Daily 10:00 - 4:00, 408-292-8188, Kids under $1
ROSICRUCIAN PARK MUSEUM & PLANETARIUM (science exhibits, Egyptian collection, planetarium shows), 1342 Naglee Ave., Daily 9:00 - 5:00 (Saturday, Sunday, Monday, 12:00 - 5:00), 408-287-9117, Museum free, Kids (for planetarium) under $1

SANTA ANA
MOVIELAND OF THE AIR MUSEUM (over 50 antique & restored airplanes), Orange County Airport, Summer: Daily 10:00 - 5:00, 714-545-1193, Kids (under 12) less than $1

SANTA BARBARA
MISSION SANTA BARBARA (early 1800's preserved mission, art displays, tours), East Los Olivos & Laguna Sts., Daily 9:30 - 5:00, Sunday 1:00 - 5:00, 805-682-4713, Kids (under 16) free
SANTA BARBARA CHILD'S ESTATE ZOO (farm animals, petting area, train ride, picnicking), 1300 E. Cabrillo Blvd., Daily 10:00 - 5:00 (closed Monday), 805-962-5339, Kids under $1

SOLEDAD
PINNACLES NATIONAL MONUMENT (spirelike rock formations 500 to 1,200 feet high, caves, hiking trails, picnicking), US 101, Daily 8:00 - 5:00, 408-389-4578, Vehicle use fee charged

THREE RIVERS
SEQUOIA & KINGS CANYON NATIONAL PARKS (great groves of giant sequoias, High Sierra scenery, mountain wilderness, Crystal Cave, visitor center, picnicking), Hwy. 180, Rt. 198, Summer: Daily 8:00 - 8:00, 209-565-3351, Vehicle use fee charged

COLORADO

ALAMOSA
GREAT SAND DUNES NATIONAL MONUMENT (among largest & highest dunes in country, self-guiding trails, visitor center, picnicking), US 160, Summer: Daily 7:00 - 8:00, 303-378-2312, Vehicle use fee charged

COLORADO SPRINGS
CHEYENNE MOUNTAIN ZOOLOGICAL PARK (over 1,000 animals, birds & reptiles, tours), Broodmoor-Cheyenne Mt. Highway, Summer: Daily 9:00 - 6:00, 303-633-3522, Kids (under 6) free
HALL OF PRESIDENTS WAX MUSEUM (historical scenes, presidents, first ladies), 1050 S. 21st St., Summer: Daily 9:00 - 6:00, 303-635-3553
HOUSE OF CAR (antique autos), 1102 S. 21st St., Summer: Daily 9:00 - 5:00, 303-473-7776
PIKES PEAK GHOST TOWN (realistic Old-West town, general store, saloon, museum), 400 S. 21st St., Summer: Daily 9:00 - 6:00, 303-635-3553, Kids under $1

DENVER
DENVER MUSEUM OF NATURAL HISTORY (planetarium, Indian collection, picnicking), City Park, Daily 9:00 - 4:30, Sunday, Holidays, 12:00 - 4:30, 303-399-0870, Museum free, Kids (for planetarium) under $1
DENVER ZOOLOGICAL GARDENS (natural habitat exhibits, baby animals, petting area, picnicking), City Park, Summer: Daily 10:00 - 6:00, 303-297-2754, Kids (under 15) free
FORNEY TRANSPORTATION MUSEUM (over 200 antique vehicles, costumed manikins, films), 1416 Platte St., Daily 9:00 - 6:00, 303-433-3643, Kids under $1

ESTES PARK
MOVIE MUSEUM (Hollywood via films, wax figure scenes, memorabilia), US 66 (Fun City), Summer: Daily 10:00 - 10:00, 303-586-3607
ROCKY MOUNTAIN NATIONAL PARK (over 100 named peaks over 10,000 feet high, self-guided trails, visitor center, museum, picnicking), Rt. 66, Daily 8:00 - 5:00, Vehicle use fee charged

FAIRPLAY
SOUTH PARK CITY MINING TOWN (restored Old-West mining town,
tours), Rt. 285 to Front St., Summer: Daily 9:00 - 7:00, 303-836-2387,
Kids under $1

GOLDEN
COLORADO RAILROAD MUSEUM (turn-of-the-century railroad station,
steam locomotives, railroad equipment, picnicking), 17155 W. 44th Ave.
(Rt. 58), Daily 9:00 - 5:00, 303-279-4591, Kids under $1

MANITOU SPRINGS
COLORADO CAR MUSEUM (antique autos), US 24, Summer: Daily
9:00 - 9:00, Sunday 1:00 - 9:00, 303-685-5996, Kids under $1

MESA VERDE NATIONAL PARK
MESA VERDE NATIONAL PARK (best preserved prehistoric cliff dwell-
ings in the USA, guided tours, visitor center, museum, picnicking), US 160
(Cortez), Daily 8:00 - 5:00, 303-529-4475, Vehicle use fee charged

MONTROSE
BLACK CANYON OF THE GUNNISON NATIONAL MONUMENT
(sheer-walled canyon, over 13,000 acres, visitor center, picnicking), US 50,
Daily sunrise - sunset, Vehicle use fee charged
COLORADO NATIONAL MONUMENT (towering monoliths, sheer-walled
canyons, over 17,000 acres, self-auto tour, wildlife, visitor center, picnick-
ing), Rt. 340 (Grand Junction), Summer: Daily 8:00 - 8:00, 303-858-3617,
Vehicle use fee charged

CONNECTICUT

BRIDGEPORT
BARNUM MUSEUM (circus memorabilia, 50,000 piece hand-carved model
circus), 820 Main St., Daily 12:00 - 5:00, Saturday 2:00 - 5:00 (closed
Monday), 203-576-7320, By donation
MUSEUM OF ART, SCIENCE & INDUSTRY (planetarium, paintings,
furniture, Indian items), 4450 Park Ave., Daily 2:00 - 5:00 (closed Monday), 203-372-3521, Museum by donation, Kids (for planetarium) under $1

BRISTOL
AMERICAN CLOCK & WATCH MUSEUM (almost 2,000 timepieces, antiques, grandfather clocks), 100 Maple St., Summer only: Daily 1:00 - 5:00
(closed Monday), 203-583-6070, Kids (under 8) free

EAST HADDAM
GILLETTE CASTLE STATE PARK (preserved castle, over 20 rooms,
picnicking), Hwy. 82, Summer only: Daily 11:00 - 5:00, 203-526-2336,
Kids under $1

EAST HAVEN (New Haven)
BRANFORD TROLLEY MUSEUM (almost 100 trolley cars, antiques, exhibits, rides, picnicking), US 1 to 17 River St., Summer: Daily 11:00 - 5:00,
203-467-6927, Kids (under 5) free

FARMINGTON
FARMINGTON MUSEUM/STANLEY WHITMAN HOUSE (preserved
17th-century house, garden), 37 High St., Summer: Daily 2:00 - 5:00
(closed Monday) Saturday 10:00 - 12:00 & 2:00 - 5:00, 203-677-9222, Kids
under $1
HILLSTEAD MUSEUM (historical mansion, art exhibits), Mountain Rd.,
Wednesday, Thursday, Weekends 2:00 - 5:00, 203-677-9064, Kids under $1

GREENWICH
MUSEUM OF CARTOON ART (exhibits, lectures), 384 Field Point Rd., Daily 10:00 - 4:00 (closed Monday), 203-661-4502, Kids under $1

HARTFORD
BUTLER-McCOOK HOMESTEAD (18th-century preserved home, exhibits), 396 Main St., Summer: Daily 12:00 - 4:00 (closed Monday, Wednesday), 203-522-1806, Kids under $1
HARRIET BEECHER STOWE HOUSE (restored author's home, visitor center), Nook Farm, 77 Forest St., Summer: Daily 10:00 - 4:00, 203-525-9317, Kids under $1
MARK TWAIN MEMORIAL (Mr. Twain's preserved home), 351 Farmington Ave., Summer: Daily 10:00 - 4:00, 203-525-9317, Kids under $1
NOAH WEBSTER HOUSE (18th-century preserved home, gardens, exhibits), 227 S. Main St., Tuesday, Thursday, Sunday 1:00 - 4:00, 203-521-1939, Kids (under 6) free

MYSTIC
DENISON HOMESTEAD (restored historic museum, colonial exhibits, tours), Pequotsepos Rd., Summer: Daily 1:00 - 5:00 (closed Monday), 203-536-9246, Kids under $1
DENISON PEQUOTSEPOS NATURE CENTER (museum, nature trails, exhibits), Pequotsepos Rd., Daily 9:00 - 5:00, Sunday 1:00 - 5:00, (closed Monday), 203-536-1216, Under $1
MEMORY LANE DOLL & TOY MUSEUM (toy & doll exhibits, antiques), I-95, Hwy. 27, Daily 10:00 - 6:00, 203-536-3450, Under $1

NEW HAVEN
PEABODY MUSEUM (natural history museum, exhibits, 70 foot brontosaurus), Yale University, 170 Whitney Ave., Daily 9:00 - 5:00, Sunday 1:00 - 5:00, 203-432-4044, Under $1

STAMFORD
STAMFORD MUSEUM & NATURE CENTER (natural history museum, planetarium, dairy farm, zoo, picnicking), Rt. 137, Summer: Daily 9:00 - 5:00, Sunday 1:00 - 5:00, 203-322-1646, Museum & Nature Center free (Parking fee under $2.50), Kids (for planetarium) under $1

WEST HARTFORD
CHILDREN'S MUSEUM (natural history museum, planetarium, Indian items, aquarium, gardens, picnicking), 950 Trout Brook Dr., Summer: Daily 10:00 - 5:00, Sunday 1:00 - 5:00, 203-236-2961, Museum free, Planetarium shows under $2.50

DELAWARE

DELAWARE CITY (Pea Patch Island)
FORT DELAWARE STATE PARK (19th century Civil War fort, museum, trails, picnicking), located on Pea Patch Island, Summer: Daily 12:00 - 6:00 (regular schedule of boats), 302-834-7987

GREENVILLE (Wilmington)
DELAWARE MUSEUM OF NATURAL HISTORY (permanent & changing exhibits, Hall of Mammals, Hall of Birds), Hwy. 52, Daily 9:00 - 4:00, Sunday 1:00 - 5:00, (closed Monday, Tuesday), 302-658-9111, Kids (under 5) free

NEW CASTLE
AMSTEL HOUSE (restored 18th-century home, museum), The Green, 2 E. 4th St., Daily: 11:00 - 4:00, Sunday 1:00 - 4:00, (closed Monday, Tuesday), 302-322-2794 (historical society), Kids under $1
OLD DUTCH HOUSE (restored 17th-century home, museum, early Dutch exhibits), The Green, 32 E. 3rd St., Summer: Daily 11:00 - 4:00, Sunday 12:00 - 5:00 (closed Monday), 302-322-2794 (historical society), Under $1
REED HOUSE (early 1800's preserved home, guided tours, boxwood gardens), The Strand, Summer: Daily 10:00 - 5:00, Sunday 12:00 - 5:00, (closed Monday), 302-322-8411, Kids (under 6) free

WILMINGTON
DELAWARE ART MUSEUM (permanent & changing exhibits, paintings, sculpture, graphics, tours), 2301 Kentmere Pkwy., Daily 10:00 - 5:00, Sunday, 1:00 - 5:00, 302-571-9590, Kids (under 12) free

DISTRICT OF COLUMBIA

(Most major attractions in our nation's capital are free)

CORCORAN GALLERY OF ART (American art, paintings, drawings, sculpture, 18th to 20th-century art collection), 17th St., & New York Ave., N.W., Daily 11:00 - 5:00, (closed Monday), 202-638-3217, Kids (under 12) free
FRANCISCAN MONASTERY (Holy Land Of America, replicas of religious shrines), 1400 Quincy St., N.E., Daily 8:30 - 4:30, 202-526-6800, By donation
MUSEUM OF AFRICAN ART (restored townhouse of Frederick Douglass, 19th-century black abolitionist, exhibits, memorabilia), 316 "A" St., N.E., Daily 11:00 - 5:00, Weekends 1:00 - 5:00, 202-547-7424, By donation
NATIONAL COLONIAL FARM (located in Maryland, mid-1700's working farm), Rt. 210 (Maryland) to Brian Point Rd., Summer: Daily 10:00 - 5:00 (closed Monday), 301-283-2113, Kids under $1
NATIONAL ZOOLOGICAL PARK (over 2,000 animals, birds & reptiles, indoor & outdoor exhibits, giant pandas, train ride, picnicking), Rock Creek Park, Connecticut Ave. & Harvard St., Summer: Daily 9:00 - 6:30, 202-381-7228, Zoo free, Parking fee
WASHINGTON MONUMENT (over 500 feet high obelisk, observation area), The Mall, 14th-17th Street, N.W., Summer: Daily 8:00 - midnight, 202-426-6839, Obelisk elevator 10¢
WOODROW WILSON HOUSE (Georgian mansion, exhibits, memorabilia, garden), 2340 "S" Street, N.W., Daily 10:00 - 2:00, Weekends 12:00 - 4:00, 202-387-4062, Kids under $1

FLORIDA

BRADENTON
SOUTH FLORIDA MUSEUM & BISHOP PLANETARIUM (natural history museum, Indian collection, planetarium shows), 201 10th St., W., Daily 10:00 - 5:00, Sunday 1:00 - 5:00, 813-746-4131, Kids under $1

CAPE CANAVERAL
MUSEUM OF SUNKEN SPANISH TREASURE (treasure from sunken fleet, exhibits), 8625 Astronaut Blvd., Daily 9:30 - 5:15, 305-783-8573, Kids (under 6) free

CLERMONT
CITRUS TOWER (200 feet high observation tower, exhibits), US 27, Daily 7:30 - sunset, 904-394-2145, Kids (under 10) free

DAYTONA BEACH
MUSEUM OF ARTS & SCIENCE (planetarium, paintings, aquarium, gardens, picnicking), 1040 Museum Blvd., Daily 9:00 - 5:00, Weekends 1:00 - 5:00, 904-255-0285, Under $1

FORT LAUDERDALE
SWIMMING HALL OF FAME (museum, exhibits), Seabreeze Blvd., Daily 10:00 - 5:00, Sunday 12:00 - 4:00, 305-334-3614, Kids under $1

FORT MYERS
THOMAS EDISON WINTER HOME (museum, laboratory, tropical garden, tours), 2350 McGregor Blvd., Daily 9:00 - 4:00, Sunday 1:00 - 4:00, 813-334-3614

FORT WALTON BEACH
INDIAN TEMPLE MOUND MUSEUM (historical site, dioramas, exhibits), US 98, Daily 11:00 - 4:00 (closed Monday), 904-243-6521, Under $1

HOMESTEAD
CORAL CASTLE (one of Americas most unusual castles, built entirely of coral by one man, carved coral furnishings, garden, tours), US 1, Daily 9:00 - 5:00, 305-248-6344, Kids (under 6) free
EVERGLADES NATIONAL PARK (largest remaining subtropical wilderness in USA, over 1,400,000 acres, tram tour, boat tours, self-guiding trails, visitor center picnicking), Rt. 27, Daily (visitor center 8:00 - 5:00), 305-247-6211, Vehicle use fee charged

JACKSONVILLE
JACKSONVILLE ZOOLOGICAL PARK (over 1,200 animals, birds & reptiles, baby animals, petting area, kiddie rides, animal rides, picnicking), 8605 Zoo Rd., Daily 9:00 - 4:45, 904-765-4432, Kids (under 6) free

KEY BISCAYNE (Miami)
CRANDON PARK ZOO (over 1,000 animals & birds, baby animals, petting area, kiddie rides, picnicking), 4000 Crandon Blvd., Daily 9:30 - 4:30, 305-361-5421, Kids (under 16) free

KISSIMMEE
GATORLAND ZOO (crocodiles, alligators, flamingos, train tour) US 441 N., Summer: Daily 8:30 - 7:00, 305-855-5496
SST AVIATION MUSEUM (airplane exhibits, space capsule), US 192, Summer: Daily 9:00 - 8:00, 305-846-2625, Kids (under 6) free

LAKE WALES
MOUNTAIN LAKE SANCTUARY (features Edward W. Bok singing tower, carillon recitals, botanical gardens, bird observatory, picnicking), US 27, Hwy. 60, Daily 8:00 - 5:30, 813-676-1355, Parking fee

MARIANNA
FLORIDA CAVERNS STATE PARK (limestone cavern tours, museum, swimming, picnicking), Hwy. 167, Daily 8:00 - sunset, 904-482-3632, Kids (under 12) less than $1

MIAMI
HOLBROOK ARMS MUSEUM (firearms exhibits, antiques, coins, guided tours), 12953 Biscayne Blvd., Daily 10:00 - 5:30, 305-891-1806, Kids (with adult) free

VIZCAYA MUSEUM & GARDENS (housed in Renaissance-like palace, art exhibits, antiques, formal garden), 3251 S. Miami Ave., Daily 9:30 - 5:30, 305-854-3531, Kids (under 6) free

ORLANDO
JOHN YOUNG MUSEUM & PLANETARIUM (history, science, space corner, planetarium shows), Loch Haven Park, 810 E. Rollins Ave., Daily 9:00 - 5:00 Weekends, Holidays 12:00 - 5:00, 305-896-7151, Kids under $1

PALM BEACH
HENRY MORRISON FLAGLER MANSION (historical museum, early 1900's furnishings, exhibits, tours), Whitehall Way, Daily 10:00 - 5:00 (closed Monday), 305-655-2833

PALMDALE
CYPRESS KNEE MUSEUM (exhibits, tours), US 27, Daily 8 - sunset, 813-675-2951, Kids (under 12) free

ST. AUGUSTINE
CASTILLO DE SAN MARCOS NATIONAL MONUMENT (oldest masonry fort in USA, guided tours, self-guided trails), 1 Castillo Dr., Daily 8:30 - 5:00, Under $1
LIGHTNER MUSEUM (natural science, art, antiques, dolls, gardens, tours) King St., Daily 9:00 - 5:00, 904-829-9677, Kids (under 12) free
OLDEST STORE MUSEUM (late 1800's general store, blacksmith shop, antiques), 4 Artillery Lane, Daily 9:00 - 5:00, Sunday 1:00 - 5:00, 904-829-9729, Kids (under 12) free
ZORAYDA CASTLE (exhibits, antiques, tours), 83 King St., Summer: Daily 9:00 - 9:00, 904-824-3097, Kids (under 6) free

ST. PETERSBURG
MGM BOUNTY (MGM sailing ship, Tahitian scene, exhibits), 345 2nd Ave., N.E., Daily 9:00 - 10:00, 813-896-3117
ST. PETERSBURG HISTORICAL MUSEUM (science, natural history, Americana, tours), 335 2nd Ave., N.E., Daily 11:00 - 5:00, Sunday 1:00 - 5:00, 813-894-1052, Kids (under 5) free
ST. PETERSBURG MUSEUM OF FINE ARTS (paintings, sculpture, photography, films, tours) 255 Beach Dr., N., Daily 10:00 - 5:00, Sunday 1:00 - 5:00, (closed Monday), 813-896-2667, By donation

SARASOTA
MARIE SELBY BOTANICAL GARDENS (over 5 acres, greenhouse), 800 S. Palm Ave., Daily 10:00 - 5:00, 813-366-5730, Kids (under 16) free

STUART (Hutchinson Island)
ELLIOTT MUSEUM (antique vehicles, memorabilia), Hutchinson Island, 888 N.E. McArthur Blvd., Daily 1:00 - 5:00, 305-287-4256, Kids under $1
HOUSE OF REFUGE (restored historical site, aquarium), Hutchinson Island, Ocean Blvd., Daily 1:00 - 5:00, 305-287-4392, Kids under $1

WEST PALM BEACH
DREHER PARK SCIENCE MUSEUM & PLANETARIUM (exhibits, planetarium shows), Dreher Park, Lakewood Rd., Daily 10:00 - 5:00, Sunday 1:00 - 5:00 (closed Monday), 305-832-1988, Under $1
DREHER PARK ZOOLOGICAL GARDENS (picknicking), Dreher Park, Summit Blvd., Daily 9:00 - 5:00, 305-585-8697, Kids under $1

WINTER HAVEN
MUSEUM OF OLD DOLLS & TOYS (antique dolls & toys), 1530 6th St., N.W., Daily 10:00 - 6:00, Sunday, Holidays 12:00 - 5:00, 813-299-1830, Kids (under 8) free

WINTER PARK
BEAL-MALTBIE SHELL MUSEUM (extensive shell collection), Rollins College, Holt Ave., Summer only: Daily 10:00 - 5:00, Tuesday - Sunday 1:00 - 5:00 (closed Monday), 305-646-2364, Kids under $1

GEORGIA

ATHENS
TAYLOR-GRADY HOME (preserved 19th-century home, antiques, exhibits), 634 Prince Ave., Monday, Wednesday, Friday 10:00 - 2:00, Sunday 2:00 - 5:00, 404-549-8688

ATLANTA
ATLANTA ZOOLOGICAL PARK (animal & bird exhibits, petting area, children's zoo, kiddie rides, picnicking), Grant Park, Daily 10:00 - 5:00, 404-622-4839, Kids (under 6) free
CYCLORAMA (the battle of Atlanta), Grant Park, Daily 10:00 - 5:00, 404-658-6374
FERNBANK SCIENCE CENTER (museum, observatory, planetarium shows, nature trails, gardens), 156 Heaton Park Dr., N.E., Daily 10:00 - 4:00, 404-378-4311, Fernbank: Free (fee for planetarium)
WREN'S NEST — THE JOEL CHANDLER HARRIS MEMORIAL (preserved historical home, period furnishings, memorabilia), 1050 Gordon St., S.W., Daily 10:00 - 5:00, Sunday 2:00 - 5:00, 404-753-8535, Kids under $1

AUGUSTA
MEADOW GARDEN (18th-century historic home, exhibits), 1320 Nelson St., Tuesday, Thursday, Saturday 1:00 - 4:00, 404-724-4174, Kids (under 12) less than $1

BLAKELY
KOLOMOKI MOUNDS STATE HISTORICAL PARK (Indian museum, burial grounds, picnicking), US 27, Park: Daily 7:00 - 10:00, 912-723-5296, Under $1

CRAWFORDVILLE
ALEXANDER H. STEPHENS MEMORIAL PARK — LIBERTY HALL (restored historical home, museum, exhibits, regional items, picnicking), Hwy. 47, Park: Daily 7:00 - 10:00, 404-456-2221, Under $1

MACON
CANNON BALL HOUSE (mid 19th-century home, Civil War museum, regional items), 856 Mulberry St., Daily 10:30 - 4:30, Weekends 1:30 - 4:30, 912-745-5982, Kids under $1
HAY HOUSE (Renaissance-style home, exhibits, antiques), 934 Georgia Ave., Daily 10:30 - 4:30, Weekends 1:30 - 4:30, 912-742-8155, Kids (under 5) free
MUSEUM OF ARTS & SCIENCES (paintings, sculpture, nature center, planetarium shows, observatory, nature trails), 4182 Forsyth Rd., Daily 9:00 - 5:00, Saturday 11:00 - 5:00, Sunday, 2:00 - 5:00, 912-477-3232, Under $1 (fee for planetarium)

SAVANNAH
DAVENPORT HOUSE (early 1800's restored home, period furnishings, antiques), 324 E. State St., Daily 10:00 - 4:30 (closed Sundays, Holidays), 912-236-8097, Kids (under 10) free
FORT PULASKI NATIONAL MONUMENT (early 19th-century fort, visitor center, picnicking), US 80, Summer: Daily 8:30 - 6:00, 912-786-5787, $1 per car

OWENS-THOMAS HOUSE MUSEUM (19th-century home, garden), 124 Abercorn St., Daily 10:00 - 5:00, Sunday, Monday 2:00 - 5:00, 912-233-9743, Kids (under 6) free

SAVANNAH SCIENCE MUSEUM (planetarium, aquarium, regional exhibits), 4405 Paulsen St., Daily 10:00 - 5:00, Sunday 2:00 - 5:00, (closed Monday), 912-355-6705, Kids (under 12) less than $1

SHIPS OF THE SEA MUSEUM (sailing-ship models, nautical memorabilia), 503 E. River St., Summer: Daily 10:00 - 5:00, 912-232-1511, Kids (under 7) free

TELFAIR ACADEMY OF ARTS & SCIENCES (art museum, paintings, sculpture, drawings, tours), 121 Barnard St., Daily 10:00 - 4:40, Sunday 2:00 - 5:00 (closed Monday), 912-232-1177, Kids under $1

WARM SPRINGS

FRANKLIN D. ROOSEVELT'S LITTLE WHITE HOUSE (historic site museum, Roosevelt memorabilia, films, picnicking), US 27, Daily 9:00 - 5:00, 404-655-3511, Kids (under 6) free

HAWAII

HILO

LYMAN HOUSE (19th-century historic house, period furnishings, museum, tours), 276 Haili St., Daily 10:00 - 4:00 (closed Sunday), 808-935-5021, Kids under $1

HONOLULU

BISHOP MUSEUM (natural history museum, anthropology, archaeology & zoology collections), 1355 Kalihi St., Daily 9:00 - 5:00, Sunday 12:00 - 5:00, 808-847-1443, Kids (under 18) free

HONOLULU ACADEMY OF ARTS (Eastern & Western art collection, Chinese garden, tours), 900 S. Beretania St., Daily 10:00 - 4:30, Sunday 2:00 - 5:00, Kids (under 12) free

HONOLULU ZOO (baby animals, petting area, botanical garden, tours, picnicking), 151 Kapahulu Avenue, Daily 9:00 - 5:00, 808-923-7723

QUEEN EMMA SUMMER PALACE (mid 19th-century historic house museum, period furnishings, memorabilia, tours), 2913 Pali Hwy., Daily 9:00 - 4:00, Saturday 9:00 - 12:00 (closed Sunday), 808-595-3167, Kids under $1

WAIKIKI AQUARIUM (tropical fish collection, seals, permanent exhibits), 2777 Kalakaua Ave., Daily 10:00 - 5:00, 808-923-9741, Kids (under 16) free

KAILUA KONA

HULIHEE PALACE (19th-century historical house museum, authentic furnishings, tours), Alii Drive, Daily 10:00 - 4:00, 808-329-1877, Kids (under 12) less than $1

WAILUKU

HALE HOIKEIKE (early 19th-century historical house, early Hawaiian artifacts, museum, tours), Iao Road, Daily 10:00 - 3:30 (closed Sunday), 808-244-3326, Kids under $1

IDAHO

AMERICAN FALLS

CRYSTAL ICE CAVES (guided cave tours, nature trails), Hwy. 39, North Pleasant Valley Rd., Summer only: Daily 9:00 - 6:00, 208-226-2465, Kids (under 6) free

ARCO
CRATERS OF THE MOON NATIONAL MONUMENT (fissure eruptions, crater, volcanic cones, lava flows, visitor center, self-guided trails, picnicking), US 93, Summer: Daily 8:00 - 8:00, 208-527-3257, $1 per car

BLACKFOOT
BINGHAM COUNTY MUSEUM (regional & Indian items), 190 N. Shilling St., Daily, 208-785-1330, By donation

BOISE
BOISE ART GALLERY (regional & European exhibits), Julia Davis Park, Daily 10:00 - 5:00, Weekends 12:00 - 5:00, 208-345-8330
JULIA DAVIS ZOO (children's zoo, petting area, kiddie rides, picnicking), US 30, Daily 10:00 - 5:00, 208-383-4230, Under $1

IDAHO FALLS
INTERMOUNTAIN SCIENCE EXPERIENCE CENTER (exhibits, experiments, demonstrations), Science Center Dr., Daily 10:00 - 4:00, 208-524-1776, Kids (under 6) free
TAUTPHAUS PARK ZOO (animal & bird exhibits, kiddie rides, picnicking), I-15, Daily 9:00 - 5:00, 208-529-1470, Under $1

MONTPELIER
MINNETONKA CAVE (guided cave tours), US 89 (St. Charles), Summer: Daily 10:00 - 5:00, Kids (under 6) free

MOSCOW
LATAH COUNTY HISTORICAL MUSEUM (regional items, dioramas), 110 South Adams St., Daily 9:00 - 4:00, Weekends 1:00 - 4:00, 208-882-1004

SHOSHONE
SHOSHONE INDIAN ICE CAVES (guided cave tours, Indian museum), US 93, Summer only: Daily 8:00 - 8:00, Kids (under 6) free

TWIN FALLS
TWIN FALL HISTORICAL SOCIETY MUSEUM (Old-West scene, antiques, memorabilia), US 30, 90, Summer: Daily 10:00 - 5:00, Sunday 2:00 - 5:00, Under $1

ILLINOIS

AURORA
AURORA HISTORICAL MUSEUM (mid 19th-century home, Indian & regional exhibits), 304 Oak Ave., Wednesday & Sunday, 2:00 - 4:30, 312-897-9029, By donation
PIONEER PARK (old-fashioned farming community scene, museum, rides, zoo, regional animal & bird exhibits, picnicking), Galena & Barnes Rd., Summer only: Daily 10:00 - 6:00, 312-892-1550, Under $1

BLOOMINGTON
MILLER PARK'S ZOO (native animal exhibits, petting area, picnicking), 1020 S. Morris Ave., Summer: Daily 10:00 - 7:00, 309-829-7961

BROOKFIELD (Chicago)
BROOKFIELD ZOOLOGICAL GARDENS (natural habitat exhibits, animals, birds & reptiles, sea shows, children's zoo, baby animals, train ride, gardens, picnicking), I-90, I-55 exit 1st Ave. at 31st Street, Summer: Daily 10:00 - 6:00, 312-242-2630, Kids (under 6) free, Parking fee

CHICAGO
ART INSTITUTE OF CHICAGO (paintings, sculpture, drawings, decorative arts, miniature period rooms, junior museum), Michigan Ave., Adams St., Daily 10:30 - 4:40, Sunday 12:00 - 5:00, 312-443-3600
CHICAGO HISTORICAL SOCIETY (museum, local & regional items, period rooms, reference library, tours), Lincoln Park, Daily 9:30 - 4:30, Sunday 12:00 - 5:00, 312-642-4600, Kids (under 6) free
FIELD MUSEUM OF NATURAL HISTORY (one of the world's biggest natural science museums, primitive arts, Indian collection, dioramas, precious stones), Grant Park, US 41, Summer: Daily 9:00 - 6:00, 312-922-9410, Kids under $1
JOHN SHEDD AQUARIUM (1,000's of sea creatures, coral reef scene, penguins, piranhas, sea horses), Grant Park, Summer: Daily 9:00 - 5:00, 312-939-2426, Kids under $1
SEARS TOWER (world's tallest building, observation deck), 233 S. Wacher Dr., Daily 9:00 - midnight, Toddlers (under 2) free

DECATUR
SCOVILL PARK ZOO (children's zoo, petting area, farm animals, picnicking), South Country Club Rd., Summer: Daily 1:00 - sunset, 217-422-1712, Under $1

FREEPORT
STEPHENSON COUNTY HISTORICAL SOCIETY MUSEUM (includes pioneer farm museum, country schoolhouse, arboretum), 1440 S. Carroll Ave., Summer: Friday, Saturday, Sunday, 1:30 - 5:00, 815-232-8419, By donation

LISLE
MORTON ARBORETUM (nature trails, ponds, visitor center, picnicking), Hwy. 53, Daily 9:00 - 5:00, 312-968-0074, $1 per car

PEORIA
GLEN OAK PARK ZOO (petting area, kiddie rides, botanical garden, picnicking), Prospect Rd., Summer: Daily 10:00 - 4:00, 309-682-2534, Kids (under 6) free

ROCKFORD
CHILDREN FARM (feeding & petting areas, pony rides), 5209 Safford Rd., Summer: Daily 11:00 - 5:00, 815-964-8054, Under $1
TINKER SWISS CHALET (built in late 19th-century, historical & regional exhibits), 411 Kent St., Wednesday - Sunday 2:00 - 4:00, 815-964-2424, Kids (under 6) free

SPRINGFIELD
LINCOLN & HERNDON LAW OFFICE BUILDING (historical museum, Lincoln's office, period exhibits), 6th & Adams St., Daily 9:30 - 5:00, 217-523-1010, Kids under $1
LINCOLN MARRIAGE HOME (Lincoln's life museum, over 25 dioramas, period furnishings), 406 South 8th St., Summer: Daily 9:00 - 5:00, 217-544-0495, Under $1
THOMAS REES MEMORIAL CARILLON (one of the biggest carillons in the world, 66 bells, 3 observation decks, guided tours), Washington Park, Daily tours Summer 2:00 - 8:00, Under $1

INDIANA

AURORA
HILLFOREST (mid 19th-century mansion, period furnishings, Ohio River views), 213 5th St., Summer: Daily 10:00 - 5:00 (closed Monday), 812-926-0121, Kids (under 12) free

BATESVILLE
WHITEWATER CANAL STATE MEMORIAL (14 mile long canal restoration, gristmill museum, picnicking), US 52 S. (Metamora) Daily (museum) 9:00 - 5:00, 317-647-6512, Under $1

CORYDON
CORYDON CAPITOL STATE MEMORIAL (early 1800's restored courthouse, historical museum, exhibits), Old Capitol Ave., Daily 9:00 - 5:00, 812-738-4890, Kids (under 12) free

ELKHART
RUTHMERE (early 1900's historical mansion, museum, period furnishings, garden, guided tours), 302 E. Beardsley St., Summer: Tuesday - Friday (tours) 11:00 A.M., 1:00 P.M., 3:00 P.M.

EVANSVILLE
ANGEL MOUNDS STATE MEMORIAL (prehistoric Indian mounds, reconstructed area, archeological exhibits, interpretive center), Rt. 662, Daily 9:00 - 5:00, 812-853-3956, Kids (under 12) free
MESKER PARK ZOO (natural habitat exhibits, over 500 animals, birds, & reptiles, petting zoo, baby animals, picnicking), Bement Ave., Summer: Daily 9:00 - 5:00, 812-426-5610, Under $1

FORT WAYNE
FORT WAYNE (historic reconstruction, exhibits), 221 S. Barr St., Summer: Daily 9:00 - 6:00, 219-424-3476, Kids (under 6) free
FRANKE PARK CHILDREN'S ZOO (baby animals, petting area, rides, picnicking), 3411 Sherman St., Summer: Daily 9:00 - 5:00, 219-483-7914, Kids under $1

GENEVA
AMISHVILLE USA (Amish farm, tours, wagon rides, picnicking), US 27, Amish Rd., Summer: Daily 9:00 - 5:00, 219-589-3536, Kids (under 6) free
LIMBERLOST STATE MEMORIAL (preserved 14 room cabin, furnishings, memorabilia) US 27, Summer: Daily 9:00 - 5:00, Sunday 1:00 - 5:00, 213-368-7428, Under $1

INDIANAPOLIS
BENJAMIN HARRISON HOME (restored late 19th-century home, furnishings), 1230 N. Delaware St., Daily 10:00 - 4:00, Sunday 12:00 - 4:00, 317-631-1898, Kids under $1
INDIANAPOLIS ZOOLOGICAL GARDENS (natural habitat exhibits, children's zoo, petting area, animal shows, rides, picnicking), George Washington Park, Summer: Daily 10:00 - 5:00, 317-547-3577, Kids (under 11) less than $1
JAMES WHITCOMB RILEY HOME (preserved historical home, tours), 528 Lockerbie St., Daily 10:00 - 4:00, Sunday 12:00 - 4:00, Kids (under 12) free

JEFFERSONVILLE
HOWARD STEAMBOAT MUSEUM (steamboat models, memorabilia, tours), 1101 E. Market St., Daily 10:00 - 4:00, Sunday 1:00 - 4:00, 812-283-3728, Kids under $1

LAFAYETTE
COLUMBIAN PARK ZOO (petting area, rides, picnicking), 1915 Scott St., Summer: Daily 12:30 - 9:00 P.M., 317-447-0133, Under $1

MADISON
J.F.D. LANIER STATE MEMORIAL (mid 19th-century restored mansion),
Elm St., Daily 9:00 - 4:00, 812-265-3526, Under $1

MICHIGAN CITY
INTERNATIONAL FRIENDSHIP GARDENS (includes bird sanctuary),
US 12, Summer: Daily 9:00 - sunset, Kids (under 6) free
WASHINGTON PARK ZOO (picnicking), Washington Park, Summer:
Daily 10:00 - 8:00, 219-872-8628, Under $1

SOUTH BEND
POTAWATOMI PARK ZOO (petting area, conservatories, picnicking),
Mishawaka Ave., Summer: Daily 10:00 - 6:00, 219-288-8133, Under $1
STORYLAND ZOO (petting area, kiddie rides, nature center, picnicking),
1304 W. Ewing Ave., Summer: Daily 12:00 - 8:00 P.M., 219-252-2366,
Under $1

VINCENNES
HARRISON MANSION — GROUSELAND (early 19th-century restored
residence), Scott & Park St., Daily 9:00 - 5:00, 812-882-3096, Kids (under
6) free
SONOTABAC INDIAN MOUND (prehistoric Indian mound, museum, regional items), 2401 Wabash Ave., Summer: Daily 1:00 - 5:00, Under $1

IOWA

AMANA COLONIES
AMANA HERITAGE HOUSE MUSEUM (Amana Colonies' history, heir-
looms, arts & crafts), Rt. 220, Daily 10:00 - 5:00, Sunday 12:00 - 5:00,
Kids under $1

COUNCIL BLUFFS
GENERAL DODGE HOUSE (mid 19th-century mansion, period furnishings, memorabilia), 605 3rd St., Daily 10:00 - 5:00, Sunday 2:00 - 5:00
(closed Monday), Kids under $1

DAVENPORT
FEJERVARY PARK'S CHILDREN'S ZOO (Mother Goose setting, petting
area, monkey island, animal rides, picnicking), Wilkes Ave., Summer: Daily
10:00 - 5:00, 319-326-9831, Under $1
PUTNAM MUSEUM (natural history, regional wildlife exhibits), 1717 W.
12th St., Daily 9:00 - 5:00, Sunday 1:00 - 5:00 (closed Monday), 319-324-
1933, Kids under $1

DECORAH
NORWEGIAN-AMERICAN MUSEUM (Norwegian American history, arts
& crafts, pioneer items), 520 W. Water St., Summer: Daily 9:00 - 5:00,
319-382-3856, Kids under $1
WONDER CAVE (guided cave tours, picnicking), US 52, Summer: Daily
9:00 - 6:00, 319-382-4769, Kids (under 6) free

DES MOINES
DES MOINES CENTER OF SCIENCE & INDUSTRY (natural science
displays, planetarium), Greenwood Park, Daily 11:00 - 5:00, Sunday 1:00 -
5:00 (closed Monday), 515-274-4138, Kids (under 12) less than $1
DES MOINES CHILDREN'S ZOO (animals, birds, reptiles, picnicking),
7401 S.W. 9th St., Summer: Daily 9:00 - 8:00, Sunday 12:00 - 8:00 (closed
Monday), 515-283-4249, Kids (under 16) less than $1

DUBUQUE
HAM HOUSE HISTORICAL MUSEUM (pioneer & Indian artifacts, includes 1800's log cabin), 2241 Lincoln Ave., Summer: Daily, 319-583-2812, Kids (under 12) free

FORT DODGE
FORT DODGE STOCKADE (historical fort & stockade, military museum, 1800's schoolhouse), US 20, Summer: Daily 9:00 - 7:00, 515-576-3641, Kids (under 5) free

KEOKUK
KEOKUK RIVER MUSEUM — THE GEORGE M. VERITY (sternwheel towboat, regional items, picnicking), Victory Park, Summer: Daily 9:00 - 5:00, Sunday & Holidays 10:00 - 6:00, 319-524-4765, Under $1

MASON CITY
KINNEY PIONEER MUSEUM (local & regional artifacts, fossils, antiques), US 18 W. (at Municipal airport entrance), Summer: Daily 12:00 - 5:00 (closed Monday, Tuesday, & Saturday), 515-423-1258, Under $1

MUSCATINE
WEED PARK ZOO (baby animals, petting area, kiddie rides, picnicking), Rt. 22, Summer: Daily 10:00 - 5:00, 319-263-1790, Under $1

OSKALOOSA
NELSON HOMESTEAD (1800's pioneer farm, outbuildings, restored log cabin, mule cemetery, craft museum), US 63, Glendale Rd., Summer: Daily 10:00 - 5:00, Sunday 1:00 - 5:00 (closed Monday), 515-672-2989, Kids (under 8) free

PELLA
PELLA HISTORIC VILLAGE RESTORATION — WYATT EARP BOYHOOD HOME (outbuildings, country store, blacksmith shop, period furnishings, antiques, museum), 507 Franklin St., Summer: Daily 9:00 - 4:30 (closed Sunday), 515-628-4311, Kids (under 13) free

SPILLVILLE
BILY CLOCK EXHIBIT (historic house museum, hand-carved clock collection, picnicking), Rt. 325, Summer: Daily 8:00 - 5:30, 319-562-3569, Kids (under 12) less than $1

WEST BEND
GROTTO OF THE REDEMPTION (over one city block in size, hourly guided tours), Rt. 15, Summer: Daily tours 8:00 - 5:00, By suggested (under $1) donation

KANSAS

ABILENE
EISENHOWER CENTER (President Eisenhower's family home, memorabilia, museum, library), 201 S.E. 4th St., Daily 9:00 - 4:45, 913-263-4751, Under $1 (kids under 15 free)
OLD ABILENE TOWN (Old-West boom town, stores, museum), I-70 & Rt. 15, Kuney St., Summer: Daily 8:00 - 8:00, 913-263-3191, By donation

BONNER SPRINGS (Kansas City)
AGRICULTURAL HALL OF FAME (history of agriculture exhibits), I-70 (Exit Bonner Springs) 630 N. 126th St., Daily 9:00 - 5:00, 913-721-1075, Kids (under 6) free

CHANUTE
SAFARI MUSEUM (African & Pacific Island relics, photographs, paintings), 16 S. Grant Ave., Daily 10:00 - 5:00, Sunday 12:00 - 6:00, 316-431-2730, Kids under $1

FORT SCOTT
FORT SCOTT NATIONAL HISTORIC SITE (early 1800's fort, visitor center, museum, restored buildings), US 69, Old Fort Blvd., Daily 10:00 - 5:00, Sunday 12:00 - 5:00, 316-223-0310, Under $1

LARNED
SANTA FEE TRAIL CENTER (history of the Santa Fe Trail), US 156, Summer: Daily 8:00 - 6:00, 316-285-2054, Kids (under 6) free

LEAVENWORTH
LEAVENWORTH COUNTY HISTORICAL SOCIETY MUSEUM (local & regional items), 334 5th Ave., Daily 1:00 - 4:30 (closed Monday), 913-682-7759, Kids (under 8) free

LINDSBORG
THE OLD MILL (historic building museum & park, pioneer items, antiques, restored buildings), 120 Mill St., Daily 9:30 - 5:00, Sunday 1:00 - 5:00, 913-227-3595, Kids (under 6) free

MEDICINE LODGE
STOCKADE MUSEUM (reconstructed 1800's stockade, log cabin, historical items), US 160, Summer: Daily 10:00 - 6:00, Sunday 1:00 - 6:00, 316-886-9982, Kids under $1

SALINA
INDIAN BURIAL SITE (prehistoric Indian burial grounds, exhibits), US 40, Daily 9:00 - 6:00, Kids under $1

SENECA
FORT MARKLEY & INDIAN VILLAGE (pioneer fort, Early-West town, stores, roaming buffalo herd, tepees, picnicking), US 36, Daily, 913-336-2285

TOPEKA
TOPEKA ZOOLOGICAL PARK (animals, birds, animal shows, picnicking), Gage Park, 10th St., Daily 9:00 - 4:45, 913-272-5821, Kids under $1

WICHITA
COW TOWN RESTORATION (late 1800's village, buildings, museum, live entertainment, picnicking), 1717 Sim Park Dr., Summer: Daily 10:00 - 7:00, 316-264-0671, Kids under $1
SEDGWICK COUNTY ZOO (natural habitat exhibits, petting area), 5555 Zoo Blvd., Summer: Daily 10:00 - 6:00, 316-942-2212, Kids (under 12) free

KENTUCKY

BARDSTOWN
WICKLAND (early 19th-century Georgian-style home, period furnishings), US 62, Summer: Daily 9:00 - sunset, 502-348-5428, Kids under $1

BOWLING GREEN
RIVERVIEW (mid 19th-century mansion, antiques), Hobson Grove Park, Summer: Daily 1:00 - 4:00, Kids (under 8) free

ELIZABETHTOWN
LINCOLN HERITAGE LOG CABIN (pioneer furnishings), Freeman Lake Park, Summer: Daily 11:00 - 6:00, Under $1

FAIRVIEW
JEFFERSON DAVIS MONUMENT (351 feet high obelisk, observatory, replica boyhood home log cabin, picnicking), US 68, Summer: Daily 9:00 - 5:00, Under $1

FRANKFORT
LIBERTY HALL (18th-century estate, period furnishings, gardens), Main St., Daily 10:00 - 5:00, Sunday 2:00 - 5:00 (closed Monday), 502-227-2560, Kids under $1
ORLANDO BROWN HOUSE (19th-century mansion, antiques), Wilkinson St., Daily 10:00 - 5:00, Sunday 2:00 - 5:00 (closed Monday), 502-875-4952, Kids under $1

LEXINGTON
ASHLAND (early 19th-century estate, heirlooms), US 25, Daily 10:00 - 4:00, Kids under $1
HOPEMONT (19th-century mansion, period furnishings, outbuildings), 201 N. Mill St., Summer: Daily 10:00 - 4:00 (closed Monday), Kids under $1
WAVELAND (historic house museum, regional items, country store, gardens), US 68, Higbee Mill Rd., Summer: Daily 10:00 - 4:00 (closed Monday), 606-272-3611, Kids (under 6) free

LOUISVILLE
AMERICAN SADDLE HORSE MUSEUM (antique carriages), 730 W. Main St., Daily 10:00 - 4:00, Sunday 1:00 - 5:00, 502-585-1342, Kids under $1
KENTUCKY RAILWAY MUSEUM (old-time trains), Eva Bandman Park, Seasonal, 502-582-9434, By donation
LOCUST GROVE (1700's country estate, period furnishings, tours), 561 Blankenbaker Lane, Daily 10:00 - 4:30, Sunday 2:00 - 4:00, 502-897-9845, Kids (under 6) free
LOUISVILLE ZOOLOGICAL GARDEN (baby animals, petting area), 1100 Trevillian Way, Summer: Daily 10:00 - 6:00, 502-459-2181, Kids under $1
MUSEUM OF NATURAL HISTORY & SCIENCE (regional exhibits, art collection), 727 W. Main St., Daily 9:00 - 5:00, Sunday 1:00 - 5:00, 502-587-3138, Kids under $1

MAMMOTH CAVE
MAMMOTH CAVE NATIONAL PARK (series of underground passages, visitor center, nature walks, Frozen Niagara tour), Hwy. 70 (Cave City), Summer: 8:00 - 7:00, 502-758-2251

OLIVE HILL
CARTER CAVES STATE PARK (nature center, Cascade Caverns, guided cave tours), US 60, Hwy. 182, Summer: Daily 9:00 - 5:00, Kids under $1

PARIS
DUNCAN TAVERN (late 1700's restored tavern, period furnishings, Anne Duncan House), 323 High St., Daily 10:00 - 5:00 (closed Monday), 606-987-1788, Kids under $1

PERRYVILLE
PERRYVILLE BATTLEFIELD (30 acre battlefield, burial grounds, battle museum, picnicking), US 68, 150, Summer: Daily 9:00 - 5:00, 606-332-8631, Kids (under 6) free

RICHMOND
WHITE HALL (18th-century estate of Cassius Marcellus Clay, noted abolitionist), Clay Lane, Summer: Daily 9:00 - 5:00, 606-623-9178, Kids under $1

SOUTH UNION
SHAKER MUSEUM (historic house museum, authentic items), US 68,
Summer: Daily 9:00 - 5:00, Sunday 1:00 - 5:00, 502-542-4167, Kids (under
6) free

LOUISIANA

AVERY ISLAND (New Iberia)
JUNGLE GARDENS (botanical gardens, bird sanctuary, Chinese Garden),
Rt. 14, Hwy. 329, Daily 8:30 - 5:00, 318-365-8173, Kids (under 6) free

BATON ROUGE
GREATER BATON ROUGE ZOO (natural habitat exhibits, kiddie rides,
tours), Greenwood Park, I-10, Daily 10:00 - 5:00, 504-775-3877, Kids (under 6) free
MAGNOLIA MOUND (1700's plantation house, period furnishings), 2161
Nicholson Dr., Daily 10:00 - 4:00, Sunday 1:00 - 4:00 (closed Monday),
504-343-4955, Kids under $1

LAFAYETTE
LAFAYETTE MUSEUM (historical house museum, Civil War items), 1122
Lafayette St., Daily 9:00 - 5:00 (closed Monday), 318-234-2208, By
donation

MANY
FORT JESUP (early 19th-century fort, period items, museum), Hwy. 6,
Daily 8:30 - 4:30, Sunday 1:00 - 4:30 (closed Monday), Kids under $1

MINDEN
GERMANTOWN MUSEUM (historical house museum, local & regional
items), US 79, Daily 10:00 - 5:00, Sunday 1:00 - 5:00 (closed Monday &
Tuesday), Kids (under 16) less than $1

MONROE
LOUISIANA PURCHASE GARDEN & ZOO (animals, birds, kiddie rides,
picnicking), US 165, Berstein Dr., Summer: Daily 10:00 - 6:00, 318-387-
1803, Kids under $1

NEW IBERIA
SHADOWS-ON-THE-TECHE (mid 19th-century restored estate, period
items, gardens), 117 E. Main St., Daily 9:00 - 4:00, 318-369-6446

NEW ORLEANS
AUDUBON PARK & ZOOLOGICAL GARDENS (botanical gardens, aquar-
ium, zoo, picnicking), St. Charles Ave., Summer: Daily 10:00 - 6:00, 504-
861-2537, Under $1
BEAUREGARD-KEYES HOUSE (mid 19th-century restored home), 1113
Chartres St., Daily 10:00 - 4:00 (closed Sunday), Kids (under 5) free
CONFEDERATE MUSEUM (Civil War items), 929 Camp St., Daily
10:00 - 4:00 (closed Sunday), 504-523-4522, Under $1
HERMANN-GRIMA HOUSE (early 1800's French Quarter home), 820 St.
Louis St., Daily 10:00 - 4:00, Sunday 1:00 - 5:00 (closed Wednesday), 504-
525-5661, Kids under $1
LOUISIANA MARITIME MUSEUM (sailing ship models), International
Trade Mart, Canal St., Daily 10:00 - 4:00 (closed Sunday), 504-581-1874,
Under $1
MADAME JOHN'S LEGACY (18th-century structure), 632 Dumaine Ave.,
Daily 9:00 - 5:00 (closed Monday), Kids (under 12) free

NEW ORLEANS MUSEUM OF ART (famous art collection), City Park, Daily 10:00 - 5:00 (closed Monday), 504-488-2631, Kids under $1
PHARMACY MUSEUM (pharmaceutical items), 514 Chartres St., Daily 10:00 - 5:00 (closed Monday), 504-524-4392, Kids under $1
PRESBYTÈRE (historic house museum), 751 Chartres St., Daily 9:00 - 5:00 (closed Monday), Kids (under 12) free

OPELOUSAS
JIM BOWIE MUSEUM (historical items), 153 W. Landry St., Daily 10:00 - 4:00 (closed Monday & Sunday), Under $1

ST. MARTINVILLE
LONGFELLOW-EVANGELINE PLANTATION (historical site museum, outbuildings, period items, picnicking), Rt. 31, 318-394-3754, Kids (under 6) free

MAINE

AUGUSTA
FORT WESTERN (18th-century restored fort, history museum), Bowman St., Summer only: Daily 9:00 - 4:00, Sunday 2:00 - 4:00, 207-622-1234, Kids (under 12) less than $1

BANGOR
BANGOR HISTORICAL SOCIETY MUSEUM (regional & Indian items), Union St., Daily 10:00 - 4:00 (closed Weekends), 207-942-5766, By donation

BETHEL
MOSES MASON HOUSE (historical house museum, antiques), 15 Broad St., Summer: Daily 1:00 - 4:00 (closed Monday), 207-633-4727, Kids under $1

BOOTHBAY HARBOR
BOOTHBAY RAILWAY MUSEUM (old-time railroad station, memorabilia, antiques, steam-train ride, picnicking), US 1 to Rt. 27, Summer: Daily 9:00 - 8:00, 207-633-4727, Kids (under 12) less than $1
GRAND BANKS SCHOONER MUSEUM (restored fishing boat, exhibits), 100 Commerce St., Summer: Daily 9:00 - sunset, 207-633-4727, Kids (under 12) less than $1
HYDE HOUSE (historic house museum, regional items), Townsend Ave., Summer: Daily 10:00 - 5:00, 207-633-2047, Under $1

CAMDEN
OLD CONWAY HOUSE (restored 18th-century farmhouse, outbuildings, regional history museum), US 1, Summer: Daily 1:00 - 5:00 (closed Weekends), 207-236-2257, Under $1

HOULTON
GALLOPS ANIMAL RANCH (regional wildlife, baby animals, petting area), US 1, Summer: Daily 10:00 - 6:00, 207-532-2020, Kids (under 3) free

KENNEBUNKPORT
SEASHORE TROLLEY MUSEUM (exhibits, memorabilia, trolley rides, picnicking), Log Cabin Rd., Summer: Daily 10:00 - 6:00, 207-967-2712

KITTERY
FORT McCLARY MEMORIAL (19th-century restored fort, picnicking), US 1 to Rt. 103, Seasonal, Under $1

LADY PEPPERRELL HOUSE (18th-century mansion, antiques), Rt. 103, Seasonal, Kids (under 12) free

PORTLAND
PORTLAND MUSEUM OF ART & McLELLAN - SWEAT HOUSE (historical house museum, exhibits, period furnishings), 111 High St., Daily 10:00 - 5:00 (closed Monday), 207-774-1822, Kids under $1
TATE HOUSE (mid 18th-century home, antiques), 1270 Westbrook St., Summer: Daily 11:00 - 5:00, Sunday 1:30 - 5:00 (closed Monday), 207-772-2023), Kids (under 12) less than $1
VICTORIA MANSION (19th-century mansion, period furnishings), 109 Danforth St., Summer: Daily 10:00 - 4:00 (closed Monday & Sunday), Kids (under 12) less than $1
WADSWORTH-LONGFELLOW HOUSE (late 18th-century residence, memorabilia), 487 Congress St., 207-774-1822, Kids (under 12) less than $1

SEARSPORT
PENOBSCOT MARINE MUSEUM (19th-century restored buildings, marine paintings, ship models, sailing charts), US 1, Summer: Daily 10:00 - 5:00, Sunday 1:00 - 5:00, 207-548-6634, Kids (under 6) free

SOUTHWEST HARBOR
MOUNT DESERT OCEANARIUM (regional sea creatures, ocean touch-tank, marine exhibits), Clark Point Rd., Summer: Daily 9:00 - 5:00 (closed Sunday), 207-244-7330, Kids (under 5) free

MARYLAND

ANNAPOLIS
HAMMOND-HARWOOD HOUSE (18th-century Georgian-style home, period furnishings, antiques), 19 Maryland Ave., Summer: Daily 10:00 - 5:00, Sunday 2:00 - 5:00 (closed Monday), 301-269-1714, Kids under 12) free

BALTIMORE
BABE RUTH BIRTHPLACE SHRINE & MUSEUM (memorabilia), 216 Emory St., Daily 10:30 - 4:00 (closed Monday, Tuesday), 301-727-1539, Kids (under 12) free
B & O TRANSPORTATION MUSEUM (railroad car collection), Pratt St. (Old Mount Clare Railroad Station), Daily 10:00 - 4:00 (closed Monday & Tuesday), 301-237-2387, Kids (under 6) free
BALTIMORE STREETCAR MUSEUM (old streetcar exhibits), 1901 Falls Rd., Seasonal, 301-727-9053, Under $1
BALTIMORE ZOO (rides, picnicking), Druid Hill Park, Daily 10:00 - 5:00, 301-396-7102, Under $1
U.S. FRIGATE CONSTELLATION (includes World War II submarine USS TORSK), City Piers & Pratt St., Summer: Daily 10:00 - 5:00, Sunday & Holidays 12:00 - 6:00, 301-539-1797, Kids (under 6) free
WASHINGTON MONUMENT (observatory), Monument St., Daily, Under $1

FREDERICK
BARBARA FRITCHIE HOUSE (historical items), West Patrick St., Daily 9:00 - 5:00, Kids (under 12) free
ROGER BROOKE TANEY HOME (historic house museum, period items, slave quarters), 121 S. Bentz St., Summer: Daily 10:00 - 4:00, Sunday 1:00 - 4:00 (closed Monday), 301-663-8687, Kids (under 12) less than $1

HAGERSTOWN
HAGER HOUSE (18th-century historic house, museum, period furnishings), City Park, Key St., Summer: Daily 10:00 - 4:00, Sunday 2:00 - 5:00 (closed Monday), 301-739-8393, Under $1 (kids under 12 free)

LAYHILL
NATIONAL CAPITAL TROLLEY MUSEUM (trolley-car exhibits, trolley ride), Hwy. 182, Seasonal, 301-384-9797, Under $1

LUTHERVILLE
FIRE MUSEUM OF MARYLAND (old-time fire trucks, antiques, tours), I-695 (Exit 26) York Rd., Seasonal, 301-321-7500, Kids (under 11) less than $1

ST. MICHAELS
CHESAPEAKE BAY MARITIME MUSEUM (local & region items, aquarium, light house), I-495 (Exit 31) Hwy. 33, Summer: Daily 10:00 - 5:00, 301-745-2916, Kids (under 6) free

WESTMINSTER
CARROLL COUNTY FARM MUSEUM (mid 19th-century farmhouse, period furnishings, outbuildings, live animals, craft demonstrations), US 140, Center St., Summer: Daily 10:00 - 4:00, Weekends 12:00 - 5:00 (closed Monday), 301-848-7775, Kids (under 6) free
UNION MILLS HOMESTEAD (18th-century historic building, period furnishings, mill museum, picnicking), US 140 N., Seasonal, 301-346-7126

MASSACHUSETTS

BOSTON
BOSTON TEA PARTY SHIP (history museum), Congress Street Bridge (Fort Point Channel), Daily 9:00 - sunset, Kids (under 5) free
BUNKER HILL MONUMENT (221 ft. high obelisk), Monument Square (Charlestown), Daily 9:00 - sunset, 617-242-3250, Under $1
FRANKLIN PARK ZOO (includes children's zoo), Blue Hill Ave., Children's zoo: Summer 10:00 - 5:00 (park zoo, Daily 10:00 - 4:00, free), 617-522-0900, Fee charged for children's zoo
JOHN HANCOCK TOWER OBSERVATORY, 200 Clarendon St., Daily 9:00 A.M. - 10:00 P.M., Sunday 12:00 - 10:00, 617-247-1976, Kids (under 15) less than $1
JOHN F. KENNEDY NATIONAL HISTORIC SITE (President Kennedy's birthplace & early boyhood home), 83 Beals St. (Brookline), Daily 9:30 - 5:00, Under $1
MUSEUM OF FINE ARTS (paintings, sculpture), 465 Huntington Ave., Daily 10:00 - 5:00 (closed Monday), 617-267-9300, Kids (under 16) free
MUSEUM OF TRANSPORTATION (antique vehicles), Larz Anderson Park (Brookline), Daily 10:00 - 5:00 (closed Monday)
PAUL REVERE HOUSE (memorabilia), 19 North Square, Summer: Daily 10:00 - 6:00, Under $1

BREWSTER (Cape Code)
CAPE CODE MUSEUM OF NATURAL HISTORY (regional wildlife exhibits, nature trails), Hwy. 6A, Summer: Daily 10:00 - 5:00, Sunday 12:30 - 5:00, 617-896-3867, Under $1
DRUMMER BOY MUSEUM (life-size paintings of the American Revolution), Hwy. 6A, Summer: Daily 9:30 - 6:00, 617-896-3823, Kids (under 4) free

CONCORD

ANTIQUARIAN SOCIETY MUSEUM (history exhibits, period rooms, memorabilia, tours), Hwy. 2A, Summer: Daily 10:00 - 4:00, Sunday 2:00 - 4:00, 617-369-9609, Kids under $1

EMERSON HOUSE (Mr. Emerson's home for almost 50 years), Hwy. 2A, Summer: Daily 10:00 - 4:00, Sunday 2:00 - 4:00, Kids (under 6) free

ORCHARD HOUSE (home of author Louisa May Alcott) Hwy. 2A, Summer: Daily 10:00 - 4:00, Sunday 1:00 - 4:00, 617-369-4118, Kids (under 6) free

DEERFIELD

HISTORIC DEERFIELD (restored village, shops, buildings, period furnishings, antiques, guided tours), US 5, Daily 9:30 - 4:30, Sunday 1:00 - 4:30, 413-773-5402

GLOUCESTER

HAMMOND CASTLE (paintings, sculpture, period furnishings, guided tours), 80 Hesperous Ave., Daily, 617-283-2080

HARVARD

FRUITLANDS MUSEUM (18th-century communal farm, outbuildings, paintings, regional & Indian items), Prospect Hill Rd., Summer: Daily 1:00 - 5:00 (closed Monday), 617-456-3924, Kids under $1

NEW BEDFORD

WHALING MUSEUM (ship models, whaling memorabilia, marine exhibits), 18 Johnny Cake Hill, Summer: Daily 9:00 - 5:00, 617-997-0046, Kids (under 6) free

PLYMOUTH

MAYFLOWER II (replica of the Pilgrims ship, period guides, exhibits), State Pier, Summer: Daily 9:00 - 8:00, 617-746-1622, Kids (under 5) free

PILGRIM HALL (history museum, memorabilia), 75 Court St., Summer: Daily 9:30 - 5:00, 617-746-1620, Kids (under 6) free

PLYMOUTH NATIONAL WAX MUSEUM (over 25 life-size historical scenes), 16 Carver St., Summer: Daily 9:00 - 9:30 P.M., 617-746-6468, Kids (under 12) less than $1

SALEM

GOULT-PICKMAN HOUSE (17th-century restored home), Charter St., Summer: Daily 10:00 - 5:00, 617-745-1638, Kids (under 6) free

PEABODY MUSEUM (natural history), Essex St., Daily 9:00 - 5:00, Sunday & Holidays 1:00 - 5:00, 617-745-1876, Kids (under 6) free

PIONEER VILLAGE (early 17th-century settlement), Forest River Park, Summer: Daily 9:00 - 6:00, 617-744-0180, Under $1

SALEM WITCH MUSEUM (witch trial scenes), Washington St., N., Summer: Daily 10:00 - 7:00, 617-744-5217, Kids (under 6) free

WITCH HOUSE (mid 17th-century structure), Essex St., Summer: Daily 10:00 - 6:00, 617-744-0180, Under $1

SPRINGFIELD

NATIONAL BASKETBALL HALL OF FAME (history of basketball exhibits), Springfield College, 460 Alden St., Summer: Daily 9:15 - 6:00, 413-781-6500, Kids (under 6) free

SPRINGFIELD ARMORY NATIONAL HISTORIC SITE (established in late 18th-century, museum, exhibits), Federal St., Daily 10:00 - 5:00, Sunday, Holidays 1:00 - 5:00, 413-732-4317, Kids (under 18) free

WORCESTER
JOHN WOODMAN HIGGINS ARMORY (firearms exhibits, armor collection), 100 Barber Ave., Daily 9:00 - 5:00, Saturday 10:00 - 3:00, Sunday 1:00 - 5:00 (closed Monday), 617-853-6015, Kids (under 5) free
WORCESTER ART MUSEUM (paintings, sculpture, tapestries, 12th-century period room), 55 Salisbury St., Daily 10:00 - 5:00, Sunday 2:00 - 5:00 (closed Monday), 617-799-4406
WORCESTER SCIENCE CENTER (planetarium, nature trails, museum, live animals, picnicking), Hwy. 9, Daily 10:00 - 5:00, Sunday 12:00 - 5:00, 617-791-9211, Kids (under 5) free

MICHIGAN

ALPENA
JESSE BESSER HISTORICAL MUSEUM (regional items, planetarium), 491 Johnson St., Summer: Daily 9:00 - 5:00, Weekends 1:00 - 5:00, 517-356-2202, Museum free, Planetarium show under $1

ANN ARBOR
KEMPF HISTORICAL HOUSE (restored mid 19th-century home, regional items), 312 S. Division St., Weekends 2:00 - 5:00, 313-761-4510, by donation

BATTLE CREEK
BINDER PARK ZOO (baby animals, petting area, picnicking), 7500 Division Dr., Summer: Daily 10:00 - 5:00, 517-979-1351, Under $1
KELLOGG BIRD SANCTUARY (visitor center, observation deck), Rt. 89, Daily 8:00 - sunset, 517-671-5721, Under $1
KIMBALL HOUSE (late 19th-century restored home, historical museum), 196 Capital Ave., N.E., Summer: Tuesday, Thursday 1:00 - 4:00, Sunday 2:00 - 4:00, 616-965-2613, Under $1
KINGMAN MUSEUM OF NATURAL HISTORY & PLANETARIUM (permanent exhibits, minerals, fossils, Discovery Room), Leila Arboretum, Daily 9:00 - 5:00 (closed Monday), 616-965-5117, Under $1

BAY CITY
MUSEUM OF THE GREAT LAKES (historical & regional items), 1700 Center Ave., Daily 10:00 - 5:00,· Weekends 1:00 - 5:00, 517-893-5733, Under $1

COPPER HARBOR
FORT WILKINS STATE PARK (restored mid 19th-century Army fort, museum, nature tours), US 41, Summer: Daily 10:00 - 4:00, 906-289-4215

DETROIT
BELLE ISLE CHILDREN'S ZOO & AQUARIUM (fairyland theme, petting area, picnicking), Island Park, Summer: Daily 10:00 - 5:00, Sunday 10:00 - 6:30, 313-398-0900, Under $1 (aquarium free)
DETROIT INSTITUTE OF THE ARTS (famous are collection, permanent & changing exhibits, period rooms), 5200 Woodward Ave., Daily 9:30 - 5:30 (closed Monday), 313-833-7900, By donation
DETROIT ZOOLOGICAL PARK (natural habitat exhibits, animal shows, petting area, rides, picnicking), Woodward Ave. (Royal Oak), Summer: Daily 10:00 - 5:00, 313-398-0903, Kids under $1 (fee charged for parking)
DOSSIN GREAT LAKES MUSEUM (ship models, paintings, marine exhibits), Island Park, Summer: Daily 10:00 - 5:00, 313-824-3157, By donation
FORT WAYNE (historic 19th-century compound, regional & Indian items), 6053 W. Jefferson Ave., May be seasonal, 313-833-9748, Kids (under 12) less than $1

GAYLORD
CALL OF THE WILD MUSEUM (nature scenes with realistic wildlife),
850 S. Wisconsin Ave., Summer: Daily 8:00 - 9:00, 517-732-4336, Kids
(under 5) free

GRAND RAPIDS
JOHN BALL ZOOLOGICAL GARDENS (petting area, aquarium, gar-
dens, picnicking), Market St., Summer: Daily 10:00 - 7:00, 616-451-0791,
Under $1

HOLLAND
BAKER FURNITURE MUSEUM (antique items), Columbia Ave., Summer: Daily 10:00 - 5:00, Sunday 1:00 - 5:00, 616-392-8761, Under $1
DUTCH VILLAGE ("Bit of Old Holland" theme, Dutch house, barn, live
animals), US 31, Summer: Daily 9:00 - sunset, 616-396-1475, Kids under $1

IRON MOUNTAIN
HOUSE OF YESTERYEAR (museum, Americana exhibits, antiques, tours),
US 2 & US 141, Summer: Daily 9:00 - 6:00, Kids (under 5) free

JACKSON
ELLA SHARP PARK FARMHOUSE & MUSEUM (regional items, planetarium, gardens, picnicking), 4th St., Summer: Daily 10:00 - 5:00, Weekends 1:30 - 5:00 (closed Monday), 517-787-2320, Under $1
MICHIGAN SPACE CENTER (U.S. space program exhibits), 2111 Em-
mons Rd., Daily 8:00 - 5:00, Monday, Weekends 11:00 - 5:00, 517-787-
4425, Kids (under 6) free

KALAMAZOO
KALAMAZOO INSTITUTE OF ARTS (20th-century art collection), 314 S.
Park St., Seasonal, 616-349-7775, By suggested (under $1) donation
KALAMAZOO NATURE CENTER (nature trails, baby animals, pioneer
homestead), North Westnedge Ave., Summer: Daily 1:00 - 5:00, 616-381-
1574, Kids under $1

LANSING
WOLDUMAR NATURE CENTER (self-guiding nature trails, wildlife),
5539 Lansing Rd., Daily, Under $1

MIDLAND
CHIPPEWA NATURE CENTER (self-guiding trails, museum, pioneer log
cabin), Hwy. 9, Daily, 517-631-0830, Under $1

OSSINEKE
DINOSAUR GARDENS (prehistoric animal museum), US 23, Summer:
Daily 8:00 - 7:00, 517-471-2181, Kids (under 12) less than $1

PORT AUSTIN
HURON CITY (pioneer buildings, general store, log cabin, period costumed
guides), Hwy. 25 E., Summer: Daily 10:30 - 5:30, Sunday 12:00 - 5:00,
Kids (under 12) free

SAULT SAINTE MARIE
S.S. VALLEY CAMP (freighter-ship tours, museum), The Locks of St.
Mary's River, I-75, US 2, Summer: Daily 9:00 - 9:00, Kids (under 6) free

MINNESOTA

ALEXANDRIA
RUNESTONE MUSEUM (home of the controversial Kensington Runestone, historic Viking artifacts, pioneer & Indian collection, agriculture
museum), 206 N. B'way, Summer: Daily 9:00 - 9:00, Kids (under 13) free

BEMIDJI
HISTORICAL & WILDLIFE MUSEUM (regional wildlife scenes, Indian & pioneer items), US 2 (in Information Center Building), Summer: Daily 8:30 - 8:30, Under $1

BRAINERD
LUMBERTOWN, U.S.A. (historical theme, 30 authentic buildings, steamboat, saw mill, live entertainment, train ride), US 371 to Rt. 77, Summer: Daily 10:00 - 6:00, 218-829-8100, Kids (under 12) less than $1

CHISHOLM
MINNESOTA MUSEUM OF MINING (history of iron mining exhibits, underground tours), US 169, Summer: Daily 8:00 - 5:00, Kids (under 11) free

DULUTH
DULUTH ZOO (animal & bird exhibits, picnicking), Rt. 23, Summer: Daily 10:00 - 8:00, 218-624-1502, Kids (under 6) free
LAKE SUPERIOR MUSEUM OF TRANSPORTATION & INDUSTRY (old-time steam locomotives & railroad car exhibits), 506 W. Michigan St., Summer: Daily 10:00 - 5:00, Sunday 1:00 - 5:00, Kids (under 6) free

EVELETH
U.S. HOCKEY HALL OF FAME (history of hockey exhibits), US 53, Rt. 37, Summer: Daily 9:00 - 8:00, 218-749-5167, Kids (under 12) less than $1

JACKSON
FORT BELMONT (reconstructed Old-West fort, outbuildings, period furnishings, antiques, tours), I-90, US 71, Summer: Daily 9:00 - 6:00, Sunday 11:00 - 6:00, Kids (under 12) free

MINNEAPOLIS
AMERICAN SWEDISH INSTITUTE (Swedish history exhibits, art collection), 2600 Park Ave., Daily 1:00 - 4:00 (closed Monday), 612-871-4907, Kids (under 6) free
IDS OBSERVATION TOWER, South 8th St., Daily 9:00 - 10:00 P.M., Weekends 9:00 - midnight, Kids (under 15) less than $1
MINNEAPOLIS INSTITUTE OF ARTS (major art collection, period rooms), 2400 3rd Ave., S., Daily 10:00 - 5:00, Sunday 12:00 - 5:00 (closed Monday) 612-870-3046, Kids (under 12) free

ST. PAUL
ALEXANDER RAMSEY HOUSE (19th-century Victorian style mansion, antiques), 265 S. Exchange St., Daily 10:00 - 4:00, Weekends 1:00 - 4:30, 612-296-2747, Kids (under 16) free
BURBANK-LIVINGSTON-GRIGGS HOUSE (late 19th-century mansion, European furnishings, antiques), 432 Summit Ave., Daily 10:00 - 4:00, Weekends 1:00 - 4:30, 612-296-2747, Kids (under 6) free
GIBBS FARM MUSEUM (late 1800's farm, outbuildings), 2097 Larpenteur Ave., W., Summer: Daily 10:00 - 5:00, Sunday 2:00 - 5:00 (closed Monday), Kids (under 16) less than $1
MINNESOTA MUSEUM OF ART, PERMANENT COLLECTION GALLERY (paintings, sculpture, drawings), 305 St. Peter St., Daily 11:00 - 5:00 (closed Monday, Sunday & August), 612-224-7431, Under $1

SHAKOPEE
STAGE COACH MUSEUM (re-created Old-West town, outbuildings, gun museum, life-size animated figures, wax museum), Rt. 101, Summer: Daily 10:00 - 9:00, 612-445-2578, Under $1

TOWER
TOWER-SOUDAN HISTORICAL MUSEUM (authentic steam engine & coach, mining exhibits), US 169, Summer: Daily 10:00 - 3:30, Under $1 (kids free)

WINONA
WILKIE STEAMBOAT MUSEUM (housed in land-bound steamboat, model boats, memorabilia), Levee Park, Summer: Daily 9:00 - 5:00, 507-452-4570, Kids under $1

MISSISSIPPI

COLUMBUS
WAVERLEY (antebellum mansion, authentic items, garden), US 45, Hwy. 50, Daily 9:00 - 6:00, Kids (under 6) free

GREENVILLE
WINTERVILLE MOUNDS (prehistoric Indian mounds, artifact museum), Hwy. 1, Daily 9:00 - 6:00 (closed Monday), 601-334-4684, Under $1

HOLLY SPRINGS
MARSHALL COUNTY HISTORICAL MUSEUM (regional history items), College Ave., Daily 8:00 - 5:00, closed Weekends, Under $1

JACKSON
JACKSON ZOOLOGICAL PARK (animal, bird & reptile exhibits, petting area), 2918 W. Capitol St., Summer: Daily 9:00 - 6:30, 601-354-5211, Under $1
MYNELLE GARDENS (over 100 varieties of trees, nature trails, lagoon), 4736 Clinton Blvd., Daily sunrise - sunset, 601-922-4011, Kids (under 12) free
THE OAKS (plantation cottage, antiques, garden), 4940 Ridgewood Rd., Daily 10:00 - 5:00 (closed Monday), 601-982-4442, Kids under $1
PETRIFIED FOREST (30 million year old stone trees, geological museum, picnicking), US 49 (Flora), Summer: Daily 9:00 - 7:00, 601-879-8189, Kids (under 6) free

MERIDIAN
MERREHOPE (antebellum estate, period furnishings), 905 31st Ave., Daily 10:00 - 5:00, Sunday 1:00 - 5:00, 601-483-8349

NATCHEZ
CONNELLY'S TAVERN (restored historical tavern, authentic furnishings), Canal St., Daily 9:00 - 5:00, 601-442-2011, Kids (under 10) free
ROSALIE (19th-century mansion, Civil War items, antiques), 100 Orleans St., Daily 9:00 - 5:00, 601-445-4555, Kids (under 10) free
STANTON HALL (elaborate antebellum estate, period furnishings, garden), 401 High St., 601-442-6282, Daily 9:00 - 5:00

PASCAGOULA
OLD SPANISH FORT (1700's fort, historic museum, regional items), 4602 Fort St., Daily 9:00 - 4:00, 601-769-1505, Kids (under 7) free

TUPELO
ELVIS PRESLEY HOME (Elvis' boyhood home, restored), Elvis Presley Park, Daily 2:00 - 5:00, Under $1

VICKSBURG
CEDAR GROVE (antebellum mansion, authentic furnishings, tours), 2200 Oak St., Daily 9:30 - 4:30, Sunday 1:30 - 4:30, 601-636-1605, Kids (under 12) less than $1

McRAVEN (historic house museum, regional items, gardens, tours), Harrison St., Summer: Daily 9:00 - 4:30, Sunday 2:00 - 4:40, 601-636-1663, Kids (under 12) less than $1
OLD COURT HOUSE (mid 19th-century structure, museum, pioneer & civil war items), 1008 Cherry St., Daily 9:00 - 4:00, Sunday 2:00 - 4:00, 601-636-0741, Kids (under 6) free

MISSOURI

BRANSON
SHEPHERD OF THE HILLS FARM (old Matt's cabin, regional history museum, Ozark arts & crafts picnicking), Rt. 76, Summer: Daily 9:00 - 7:00, 417-334-4191, Under $1 (Old Matt's cabin)

FLORIDA
MARK TWAIN'S BIRTHPLACE (writer's birthplace, museum, memorabilia), Mark Twain State Park, Hwy. 107, Summer: Daily 10:00 - 5:00, Under $1

HANNIBAL
MARK TWAIN'S BOYHOOD HOME (historical house museum, memorabilia), 208 Hill St., Summer: Daily 8:00 - 8:00, 314-221-9010, By donation
MOLLY BROWN HOUSE (19th-century mansion, antiques), 600 Prospect St., Summer: Daily 10:00 - 6:00, 314-221-8979, Under $1
ROCKCLIFFE MANSION (late 19th-century restored estate), 1000 Bird St., Daily 9:30 - 5:30, 314-221-4140, Kids (under 6) free

INDEPENDENCE
HARRY TRUMAN LIBRARY & MUSEUM (President Truman memorabilia, historical exhibits), US 24, Summer: Daily 9:00 - 7:00, 816-833-1400, Under $1
OLD JAIL (1800's restored jail, museum, outbuildings), 217 N. Main St., Summer: Daily 9:00 - 5:00, Sunday 1:00 - 5:00, 816-252-1892, Under $1
TRUMAN COURTROOM & OFFICE (historical items, restored courtroom & office), Independence Square Courthouse, Main St., Daily 9:00 - 5:00, 816-881-4467, Under $1

JEFFERSON CITY
COLE COUNTY HISTORICAL SOCIETY MUSEUM (regional items, war souvenirs), 109 Madison St., Summer: Daily 1:00 - 5:00, Wednesday 10:30 - 5:00 (closed Sunday), 314-635-1850, Kids under $1

KANSAS CITY
KANSAS CITY MUSEUM OF HISTORY & SCIENCE (regional wildlife exhibits, anthropology, Pioneer Land planetarium) 3218 Gladstone Blvd., Daily 9:00 - 5:00, Sunday 1:00 - 5:00, 816-483-8300, Museum free (fee charged for planetarium shows)
KANSAS CITY ZOO (baby animals, petting area, animal shows, picnicking), Swope Park, Daily 9:00 - 5:00, 816-333-7406, Under $1
LIBERTY MEMORIAL (217 feet high memorial shaft, observation deck, museum), Main St., Daily 9:30 - 4:30 (closed Monday), 816-274-1675, Under $1
NELSON GALLERY & ATKINS MUSEUM OF FINE ARTS (famous art collection), US 50, Daily 10:00 - 5:00, Sunday 2:00 - 6:00 (closed Monday), 816-561-4000, Under $1

LACLEDE
GENERAL PERSHING BOYHOOD HOME (historic house museum, Pershing memorabilia), US 36, Rt. 5, Summer: Daily 10:00 - 4:00, Sunday 12:00 - 6:00, 816-963-2525, Under $1

LEXINGTON
BATTLE OF LEXINGTON STATE HISTORIC SITE (major Civil War battle site, tours, picnicking), US 24, Summer: Daily 10:00 - 4:00, Sunday 12:00 - 6:00, 816-259-2112, Under $1

ST. CHARLES
BUSHNELL COUNTRY MUSEUM (pioneer village scene, shops, general store, antiques), I-70 (Exit Cave Springs), Daily 10:00 - 4:00, Under $1
FIRST MISSOURI STATE CAPITOL (19th-century restored capitol building, period furnishings), Summer: Daily 10:00 - 4:00, Sunday 12:00 - 6:00, 314-723-3256, Under $1

ST. LOUIS
BISSELL HOUSE (early 19th-century restored home), 10225 Bellefontaine Rd., Daily 10:00 - 5:00, Sunday 1:00 - 5:00, (closed Monday & Tuesday), 314-868-0973, Kids under $1
CAMPBELL HOUSE (historic house museum), 1508 Locust St., Daily 10:00 - 4:00, Sunday 12:00 - 5:00 (closed Monday), 314-421-0325, Kids under $1
CHATILLON-DE MENIL HOUSE (mid 19th-century mansion), 3352 S. 13th St., Daily 10:00 - 4:00, Sunday 1:00 - 5:00 (closed Monday), 314-771-5828, Kids under $1
JEFFERSON NATIONAL EXPANSION MEMORIAL (630 feet high Gateway Arch, observation deck, visitor center, exhibits, films), 11 N. 4th St., Summer: Daily 9:00 - 9:00, 314-425-4465, Kids under $1
MISSOURI BOTANICAL GARDENS (America's biggest botanical garden, waterfalls, lily pool, rice paddies, geodesic dome, greenhouse, picnicking), 2101 Tower Grove Ave., Summer: Daily 9:00 - 6:00, 314-772-7600, Kids under $1
ST. LOUIS SPORTS HALL OF FAME (sports history museum), Busch Stadium (Walnut St.), Summer: Daily 10:00 - 5:00, 314-421-6790, Kids under $1
USS INAUGURAL (World War II minesweeper), docked near the Jefferson National Expansion Memorial (north of the Gateway Arch), Summer: Daily 9:00 - sunset, 314-991-4616, Kids under $1

MONTANA

BROWNING
MUSEUM OF MONTANA WILDLIFE (Indian art collection, dioramas, regional items), US 2, 89, Summer: Daily 9:00 - 8:00, 406-338-4525, Kids (under 12) less than $1

BUTTE
COPPER KING MANSION (late 19th-century mansion, antiques), 219 W. Granite St., Summer: Daily 9:00 - 9:00, 406-792-7580, Kids (under 6) free

DILLON
BEAVERHEAD COUNTY HISTORICAL MUSEUM (pioneer & Indian items, picnicking), 15 S. Montana St., Summer: Daily 9:00 - 5:00, By donation

GREAT FALLS
CHARLES M. RUSSELL STUDIO (art collection, memorabilia, films, museum), 1201 4th Ave., N., Summer: Daily 10:00 - 5:00, 406-452-7369, **Kids** (under 12) free

HELENA
FRONTIER TOWN (pioneer theme, replica of Western settlement, museum), US 12, Summer: Daily 9:00 - 8:00, 406-442-4560, Kids (under 12) less than $1
GOVERNOR'S MANSION (late 19th-century mansion, period furnishings, tours), 304 N. Ewing St., Daily 9:00 - 4:00 (closed Monday)

MILES CITY
RANGE RIDERS MUSEUM (pioneer & regional artifacts), US 10, 12, Summer: Daily 9:00 - 8:00, 406-232-6146, Kids (under 12 free)

POLSON
POLSON-FLATHEAD MUSEUM (Indian collection), Main St., Summer: Daily 10:00 - 8:00, Sunday 2:00 - 8:00, By donation

RED LODGE
BIG SKY MUSEUM (historical exhibits, pioneer & Indian items), US 212, Summer: Daily 8:00 - 9:00, Kids under $1
RED LODGE ZOO (native wildlife, prairie dog town, petting area, kiddie ride), US 212, Summer: Daily 8:00 - 9:00, 406-446-2022, Kids (under 12) less than $1

STEVENSVILLE
ST. MARY'S MISSION (19th-century log mission, period & regional artifacts), US 93, Summer: Daily 10:00 - 6:00, By donation

WEST GLACIER
GLACIER NATIONAL PARK (wonderful Rocky Mountain scenery, numerous glaciers, visitor center, picnicking), US 2, US 89 (St. Mary), Summer: Daily 8:00 - 9:00, 406-888-5441, Vehicle use fee charged

WHITE SULPHUR SPRINGS
THE CASTLE (19th-century mansion, period furnishings), US 12, 89, Summer: Daily 9:00 - 9:00, 406-547-3858, Kids (under 12) free

NEBRASKA

BELLEVUE
FONTENELLE FOREST NATURE CENTER (over 1,000 acres, nature trails, ecology displays), 1111 Bellevue Blvd., Summer: Daily 8:00 - 6:00, 402-731-3140, Kids (under 12) less than $1
STRATEGIC AEROSPACE MUSEUM (aircraft & missile exhibits), 2510 Clay St., Daily 8:00 - 5:00, 402-292-2001, Kids (under 6) free

CHADRON
MUSEUM OF THE FUR TRADE (restored trading post, exhibits, pioneer & Indian items), US 20, Summer: Daily 8:00 - 6:00, 308-432-3843, Under $1 (kids free)

GERING
NORTH PLATTE VALLEY MUSEUM (regional & local items, log cabin, sod house), 11th & "J" Sts., Summer: Daily 9:00 - 5:00, Sunday 1:00 - 5:00, 308-436-4091, Kids under $1

SCOTTS BLUFF NATIONAL MONUMENT (Oregon Trail landmark, associated with 19th-century mass migration across the plains, visitor center, museum), Hwy. 92, Summer: Daily 8:00 - 8:00, 308-436-4340, Vehicle use fee charged

GRAND ISLAND
STUHR MUSEUM OF THE PRAIRIE PIONEER (restored railroad town, buildings, steam train ride, early farm machinery, antique autos), I-80, US 34, 281, Summer: Daily 9:00 - 7:00, Sunday 1:00 - 7:00, 308-384-1380, Kids under $1

HASTINGS
HASTINGS MUSEUM (natural habitat scenes, planetarium, Indian & pioneer artifacts), US 281, Daily 8:00 - 5:00, Sunday 1:00 - 5:00, 402-463-7126, Kids under $1

KEARNEY
FORT KEARNEY HISTORICAL MUSEUM (local & regional items, picnicking), 311 S. Central Ave., Summer: Daily 9:00 - 9:00, 308-234-9513, Kids (under 12) free

LINCOLN
ANTELOPE PARK CHILDREN'S ZOO (baby animals, petting area, train ride), 2800 "A" Street, Summer: Daily 10:00 - 5:00 (closed Monday), 402-475-6741, Kids (under 12) less than $1

NEBRASKA CITY
WILDWOOD PERIOD HOUSE (19th-century home, mid-Victorian items, antiques), Rt. 2, Summer: Daily 1:00 - 5:00 (closed Monday), 402-873-6340, Kids under $1

OMAHA
HENRY DOORLY ZOO (aquarium, baby animals, petting area, picnicking), Riverview Park, Summer: Daily 10:00 - 5:00, 402-733-8401, Kids under $1
JOSLYN ART MUSEUM (ancient & contemporary art collection), 2200 Dodge St., Daily 10:00 - 5:00, Sunday 1:00 - 5:00 (closed Monday), 402-342-3300, Under $1

NEVADA

BAKER
LEHMAN CAVES NATIONAL MONUMENT (limestone caverns, honeycombed by tunnels and galleries decorated with stalactites & stalagmites, visitor center, guided tours, picnicking), Rt. 74, Summer: Daily 8:00 - 5:00, 702-234-7331, Kids (under 16) free

BOULDER CITY
HOOVER DAM GUIDED TOUR (one of the world's highest dams), US 93, 466, Summer: Daily 7:30 - 7:15 P.M., 702-293-8367, Kids (under 15) free

CARSON CITY
BOWERS MANSION (mid 19th-century mansion, tours, picnicking), US 395, Summer: Daily 11:00 - 4:00, 702-849-0201, Under $1

HENDERSON
SOUTHERN NEVADA HISTORY MUSEUM (local & regional items), 240 Water St., Daily 9:00 - 4:00, Sunday 1:00 - 4:00, 702-564-5336, Under $1

RENO
FLEISCHMANN ATMOSPHERIUM & PLANETARIUM (changing shows, science exhibits), University of Nevada, North Virginia St., Daily, 702-784-4811, Kids (under 6) free

NEW HAMPSHIRE

CANTERBURY (Concord)
SHAKER VILLAGE (restored 18th-century Shaker community, period furnishings, history museum, tours), Hwy. 106, Summer: Daily 9:00 - 4:00 (closed Monday & Sunday), 603-783-9822, Kids (under 12) less than $1

CHARLESTOWN
OLD FORT NUMBER 4 (18th-century reconstructed settlement, colonial & Indian items), Rt. 11, Springfield Rd., Summer: Daily 10:00 - 5:00, 603-826-5094, Kids (under 7) free

FRANCONIA NOTCH
THE FLUME (natural wonder, waterfalls, gorge, steep grades, boardwalk, picnicking), US 3, Summer: Daily 9:00 - 6:00

FRANKLIN
DANIEL WEBSTER BIRTHPLACE (Webster memorabilia, antiques, period furnishings), Hwy. 127, Webster Rd., Summer: 9:00 - 5:00, Under $1

HILLSBORO
FRANKLIN PIERCE HOMESTEAD (President Pierce's boyhood home, memorabilia), Hwy. 127, Summer: Daily 9:00 - 5:00, Kids (under 18) free

KEENE
COLONY HOUSE (historic house museum, regional items), 104 West St., Summer: Daily 10:30 - 4:30 (closed Monday), 603-357-0889, Kids (under 12) free

NASHUA
NASHUA ARTS & SCIENCE CENTER (aquarium, science exhibits, special children's programs, children's museum), 14 Court St., Daily 10:00 - 5:00, Sunday 1:30 - 5:00, 603-883-1506, Center free (children's museum under $1)

NORTH WOODSTOCK
CLARK'S TRADING POST (amusement theme, performing bears, museum, full-size steam train ride), US 3, Summer: Daily 9:00 - 5:00, 603-745-8913, Kids (under 6) free

PORTSMOUTH
GOVERNOR LANGDON MEMORIAL (historic mansion), 143 Pleasant St., Summer: Tuesday, Thursday, Sunday 1:00 - 5:00, Kids (under 18) free
JACKSON HOUSE (17th-century preserved home), 76 Northwest St., Summer: Tuesday, Thursday, Sunday 1:00 - 5:00, Kids (under 12) less than $1
JOHN PAUL JONES HOUSE (18th-century historic house museum), 43 Middle St., Summer: Daily 10:00 - 5:00 (closed Sunday), 603-436-8420, Kids (under 6) free
MOFFATT-LADD HOUSE (late 18th-century mansion), 154 Market St., Summer: Daily 10:00 - 5:00, Sunday 2:00 - 5:00, 603-436-8221, Kids (under 6) free
WARNER HOUSE (early 18th-century Georgian-style home), 150 Daniel St., Summer: Daily 10:00 - 5:00, Sunday 2:00 - 5:00, 603-436-5909, Kids (under 6) free

WOLFEBORO
CLARK HOUSE (late 18th-century home, period furnishings, antiques),
South Main St., Summer: Daily 1:00 - 5:00 (closed Sunday), 603-569-2044,
Kids (under 6) free
LIBBY MUSEUM (regional & Indian items), North Main St., Summer:
Daily 10:00 - 5:00 (closed Monday), Under $1

NEW JERSEY

ATLANTIC CITY
ABSECON LIGHTHOUSE (restored, historic museum), Pacific & Rhode
Island Aves., Summer: Daily 10:00 - sunset, 609-292-2023, Under $1

BATSTO
WHARTON STATE FOREST RESTORED VILLAGE (18th-century re-
stored Batsto Iron Works, outbuildings, furnace, sawmill, tours), US 206,
Summer: Daily 10:00 - 6:00, Kids (under 12) free, Parking fee charged

CAMDEN
WALT WHITMAN HOME (period furnishings, Whitman memorabilia),
330 Mickle St., Daily 10:00 - 5:00, Sunday 1:00 - 6:00, Under $1

CLINTON
CLINTON HISTORICAL MUSEUM VILLAGE (1800's historic exhibits,
regional items, museum, picnicking), 56 Main St., Summer: Daily 1:00 -
5:00, Weekends 12:00 - 6:00, 201-735-4101, Kids under $1

FLEMINGTON
LIBERTY VILLAGE (1700's Americana village, museum, period crafts-
men), Church St., Daily 9:30 - 4:00, Weekends 10:30 - 5:00, 201-782-8550,
Kids (under 5) free
RAGGEDY ANN ANTIQUE DOLL & TOY MUSEUM (hundreds of dolls),
Church St., Summer: Daily 10:00 - 5:00, 201-782-1243, Under $1

FREEHOLD
MONMOUTH COUNTY HISTORICAL ASSOCIATION MUSEUM (period
rooms, antiques, attic museum), 70 Court St., Daily 10:00 - 5:00, Sunday
2:00 - 5:00 (closed Monday), 201-462-1466, Under $1
NATIONAL BROADCASTER HALL OF FAME (history of broadcasting
exhibits), West Main St., Daily 10:00 - 5:00 (closed Monday), 201-431-
4656, Kids (under 6) less than $1

MORRISTOWN
MORRISTOWN NATIONAL HISTORICAL PARK (Revolution encamp-
ment sites, Washington's headquarters, historical museum, Continental army
hospital, Ft. Nonsense), US 202, Daily 9:00 - 5:00, 201-539-2016

PATERSON
LAMBERT CASTLE (late 19th-century castle, art collection, museum),
Valley Rd. (Garret Mountain Reservation), Seasonal, 201-523-9883, Under
$1

PRINCETON
ROCKINGHAM (restored mansion, period furnishings), Rockingham State
Historic Site, Hwy. 518 (Rocky Hill), Summer: Daily 10:00 - 5:00, Sunday
1:00 - 6:00 (closed Monday & Tuesday), Under $1

TRENTON
McKONKEY FERRY MUSEUM (1700's period inn, colonial items, includes
Flag Museum), Washington Crossing State Park, Hwy. 29, Summer: Daily
10:00 - 5:00, Sunday 2:00 - 5:00, Under $1

OLD BARRACKS (1700's colonial barracks, period furnishings), South Willow St., Summer: Daily 10:00 - 5:00, Sunday 1:00 - 5:00, 609-396-1776, Under $1

TRENT HOUSE (early 18th-century home, antiques), Market St., Summer: Daily 10:00 - 5:00, Sunday 1:00 - 5:00, 609-989-3027, Under $1

WEST ORANGE

EDISON NATIONAL HISTORIC SITE (buildings & equipment used by Thomas A. Edison, period furnishings, memorabilia, films, tours), Main St., Lakeside Ave., Daily 9:00 - 4:00, 201-736-5050, Under $1

TURTLE BACK ZOO (baby animals, petting area, train ride, picnicking), Hwy. 508 (South Mountain Reservation), Summer: Daily 10:00 - 5:00, 201-731-5800, Kids under $1

NEW MEXICO

ALAMOGORDO

WHITE SANDS NATIONAL MONUMENT (white gypsum sand dunes, 10 to 45 feet high, self auto tour, visitor center, exhibits, picnicking), US 70, 82, Summer: Daily 8:00 - 7:00, 505-437-1058, Kids (under 16) free

ALBUQUERQUE

RIO GRANDE ZOOLOGICAL PARK (animals, birds, reptiles, petting area, picnicking), Rio Grande Park, Summer: Daily 10:00 - 5:00, 505-768-7823, Kids (under 16) free

AZTEC

AZTEC RUINS NATIONAL MONUMENT (prehistoric Pueblo Indian ruins, 12th-century buildings of masonry & timber, visitor center, exhibits, picnicking), US 550, Summer: Daily 8:00 - 6:00, 505-334-6754, Kids (under 16) free

CARLSBAD

CARLSBAD CAVERNS NATIONAL PARK (largest underground chambers yet discovered, visitor center, observation tower, tours, picnicking), US 62, 180, Summer: Daily 7:00 - 6:00, 505-885-8884, Kids (under 16) free

LIVING DESERT STATE PARK (botanical gardens, cactus collection, regional animal zoo, picnicking), US 285, Summer: Daily 8:00 - 10:00, 505-887-5516, Kids (under 6) free

EL MORRO

EL MORRO NATIONAL MONUMENT ("Inscription Rock" soft sandstone monolith, 100's of carved inscriptions, including 17th-century Spanish explorers, 19th-century American emigrants, visitor center, picnicking), I-40 (Grants) Hwy. 53, Summer: Daily 8:00 - 8:00 P.M., Vehicle use fee charged

HOBBS

THE FLYING MUSEUM (World War II aircraft), Hobbs Airport, US 62, 180, Summer: Daily, Kids (under 12) free

TAOS

GOVERNOR BRENT HOUSE (historic house museum, gallery), Bent St., Summer: Daily 9:00 - 5:00, 505-758-2376, Under $1

KIT CARSON HOME (1800's restored home, period furnishings, Indian items), US 64, Summer: Daily 7:30 - 7:30, 505-758-4741, Under $1

LOS ALAMOS

BANDELIER NATIONAL MONUMENT (prehistoric pueblo & cliff ruins, visitor center, self-guiding trails, picnicking), US 285 (Pojoaque) Hwy. 4 W., Summer: Daily 8:00 - 6:00, 505-672-3861, Vehicle use fee charged

MILLICENT A. ROGERS MEMORIAL MUSEUM (Spanish-style hacienda, art collection, gardens), Rt. 3, Summer: Daily 9:00 - 5:00, Sunday 1:00 - 5:00, 505-758-2462, Kids (under 6) free

TRUTH OR CONSEQUENCES
GERONIMO SPRINGS MUSEUM (Indian & pioneer artifacts), 325 Main St., Daily 10:00 - 4:00, Sunday 1:00 - 4:00, Kids (under 6) free

TUCUMCARI
TUCUMCARI HISTORICAL MUSEUM (local & regional items), 316 S. Adams St., Summer: Daily 9:00 - 8:00 P.M., Sunday 1:00 - 8:00, 505-461-3451, Kids under $1

WATROUS
FORT UNION NATIONAL MONUMENT (ruins of the key fort that shaped Southwest destiny, self-guiding trails, visitor center, exhibits, picnicking), I-25, Rt. 477, Summer: Daily 8:00 - 7:00, 505-425-8025, Vehicle use fee charged

NEW YORK

ALBANY
ALBANY INSTITUTE OF HISTORY & ART (local & regional art collection), 125 Washington Ave., Daily 10:00 - 4:45, Sunday 2:00 - 5:00, 518-463-4478, By donation

BRONX (New York City)
BRONX ZOO (one of the world's biggest zoos, animals, birds & reptiles, Wild Asia, children's zoo, animal rides, Skyfari, picnicking), Bronx Park, Summer: Daily 9:00 - 5:00, 212-933-1759, Free days: Tuesday - Thursday, Admission charged: Friday - Monday (parking fee charged)

BROOKLYN (New York City)
NEW YORK AQUARIUM (sea shows, exhibits, whale training, children's displays, picnicking), Boardwalk & West 8th St. (Coney Island), Summer: Daily 10:00 - 6:00, 212-266-8500, Kids under $1 (parking fee charged)

BUFFALO
ALBRIGHT-KNOX ART GALLERY (paintings, sculpture, period furnishings), Rt. 198, Daily 10:00 - 5:00, Sunday 12:00 - 5:00 (closed Monday), 716-882-8700, By donation
BUFFALO ZOO (animals, birds, petting & feeding area, picnicking), Delaware Park, Summer: Daily 10:00 - 7:00, 716-837-3900, Kids under $1
THEODORE ROOSEVELT INAUGURAL NATIONAL HISTORIC SITE (historic house museum, exhibits, tours), 641 Delaware Ave., Summer: Daily 10:00 - 5:00, Weekends 12:00 - 5:00, 716-884-0095, Under $1 (museum)

CANANDAIGUA
GRANGER HOMESTEAD (preserved 19th-century home, antiques, Carriage Museum), 295 N. Main St., Daily 10:30 - 5:30 (closed Monday), 315-394-1472, Kids under $1

CENTERPORT
VANDERBILT MUSEUM & PLANETARIUM (historic mansion, period furnishings, antiques, gardens), Little Neck Rd., Summer: Daily 10:00 - 4:00, Weekends 12:00 - 4:00, 516-261-5656, (planetarium 516-757-7500), Kids under $1

COOPERSTOWN
FENIMORE HOUSE (historic house museum, folk art, garden), Hwy. 80, Summer: Daily 9:00 - 5:00, 607-547-2533, Kids (under 7) free
NATIONAL BASEBALL HALL OF FAME (history of baseball exhibits, memorabilia), Hwy. 80, Summer: Daily 9:00 - 9:00, 607-547-9988, Kids (under 7) free

COXSACKIE
BRONCK HOUSE (17th-century Dutch farm, period furnishings, outbuildings, picnicking), US 9W, Summer: Daily 10:00 - 5:00, Sunday 2:00 - 6:00 (closed Monday), 518-731-8386, Kids (under 12) free

HUDSON
OLANA (19th-century castle, period furnishings, regional art collection, gardens, tours, picnicking), Rt. 9G, Summer: Daily 9:00 - 4:00 (closed Monday & Tuesday), 518-828-0135, Kids (under 12) free

NEW YORK CITY
AMERICAN MUSEUM OF NATURAL HISTORY & HAYDEN PLANETARIUM, Central Park West & 81st St., Daily 10:00 - 4:45, Sunday & Holidays 11:00 - 5:00, 212-873-1300, By donation (planetarium fee charged)
CENTRAL PARK ZOO (includes children's zoo), 5th Ave. at 64th St., Daily 10:00 - 4:30, 212-360-8288, Children's zoo 10¢
CHINESE MUSEUM (history), 8 Mott St., Daily 10:00 - 6:00, 212-964-1542, Under $1
EMPIRE STATE BUILDING OBSERVATION TOWER, 5th Ave. & 34th St., Daily 9:30 - midnight, 212-736-3100, Kids (under 12) less than $1
GUGGENHEIM MUSEUM (art), 1071 5th Ave., Daily 11:00 - 5:00 (closed Monday), 212-860-1313, Kids (under 7) free
INTERNATIONAL CENTER OF PHOTOGRAPHY (exhibits), 1130 5th Ave., Daily 11:00 - 5:00 (closed Monday), 212-860-1777, By donation
JEWISH MUSEUM (history), 1109 5th Ave., Daily 12:00 - 5:00 (closed Saturday & Jewish Holidays), 212-860-1888, Kids (under 6) free
METROPOLITAN MUSEUM OF ART, 5th Ave. & 82nd St., Daily 10:00 - 4:45, Sunday & Holidays 11:00 - 4:45 (closed Monday), 212-535-7710, By suggested (under $2.50) donation, Kids (under 12) free
MUSEUM OF AMERICAN FOLK ART, 49 W. 53rd St., Daily 10:30 - 5:30 (closed Monday), 212-581-2474, Kids (under 12) free
MUSEUM OF THE AMERICAN INDIAN (history), 155th St. & Broadway, Daily 1:00 - 5:00 (closed Monday), 212-283-2420, Kids under $1
MUSEUM OF CONTEMPORARY CRAFTS, 29 W. 53rd St., Daily 11:00 - 6:00, Sunday, Holidays 1:00 - 6:00 (closed Monday), 212-977-8989, Kids (under 12) less than $1
MUSEUM OF MODERN ART, 11 W. 53rd St., Daily 11:00 - 6:00 (closed Wednesday), 212-956-7070, Kids (under 6) free
ROCKEFELLER CENTER OBSERVATION ROOF & GUIDED TOUR, 30 Rockefeller Plaza, Summer: Daily 10:00 - 9:00, Kids (under 12) less than $1, tours daily 10:00 - 4:45, kids (under 12) less than $2.50, 212-489-2947 (no tours on Sunday)
STATUE OF LIBERTY NATIONAL MONUMENT (includes Immigration museum), Liberty Island, Daily 9:00 - 5:00, 212-732-1236, Statue (elevator 10¢) & museum free, Fee charged for round-trip boat, Kids (under 12) less than $1
THEODORE ROOSEVELT BIRTHPLACE NATIONAL HISTORIC SITE, 28 E. 20th St., Summer: Daily 9:00 - 4:30, 212-260-1616, Under $1
UNITED NATIONS GUIDED TOUR, 1st Ave. & 46th St., Daily 9:00 - 4:00 (kids under 5 not permitted on tour), 212-754-1234

WHITNEY MUSEUM OF AMERICAN ART, 945 Madison Ave., Daily 11:00 - 6:00, Sunday & Holidays 12:00 - 6:00 (closed Monday), 212-794-0600, Kids (under 12) free

WORLD TRADE CENTER OBSERVATION DECK, 2 World Trade Center, Daily 9:30 - 9:30, Kids (under 5) free

NIAGARA FALLS

NIAGARA FALLS PROSPECT POINT OBSERVATION TOWER, Prospect Park, Summer: Daily 8:00 - 11:30 P.M., Kids (under 8) free

OLD FORT NIAGARA (restored 18th-century fort, museum, period French castle, cannons, picnicking), Fort Niagara State Park (Youngstown), Prospect St., Summer: Daily 9:00 - sunset, 716-285-8254, Kids (under 12) free

OLD WESTBURY

OLD WESTBURY GARDENS (18th-century style English manor, botanical gardens, pools, trees, Georgian-style mansion, period furnishings, antiques, picnicking), 71 Old Westbury Rd., Summer: Daily 10:00 - 5:00 (closed Monday, Tuesday), 516-333-0048, Gardens: Kids (under 12) less than $1, Mansion: Kids (under 6) free

OYSTER BAY

SAGAMORE HILL NATIONAL HISTORIC SITE (Theodore Roosevelt's family estate, preserved furnishings, memorabilia, includes Old Orchard Museum), Cove Neck Rd., Summer: Daily 9:30 - 6:00, 516-922-4447, Under $1

RHINEBECK

OLD RHINEBECK AERODROME (antique plane museum, picnicking), US 9, Summer: Daily 10:00 - 5:00, Kids (under 6) free

ROCHESTER

INTERNATIONAL MUSEUM OF PHOTOGRAPHY (George Eastman House, history of photography exhibits), 900 East Ave., Daily 10:00 - 4:30 (closed Monday), 716-271-3361, Kids (under 12) less than $1

ROCHESTER MUSEUM, SCIENCE CENTER & PLANETARIUM (natural history, regional items, garden), 657 East Ave., Daily 9:00 - 5:00, Sunday, Holidays 1:00 - 5:00 (closed Monday), 716-271-4320), Kids (under 5) free

SENECA PARK ZOO (animals, birds & reptiles, petting & feeding area, rides, picnicking), 2222 St. Paul St., Summer: Daily 10:00 - 7:00, 716-266-6846, Under $1

ROME

ERIE CANAL VILLAGE & MUSEUM (mid 19th-century canal village, steam train ride, canal boat ride, picnicking), Rt. 49, New London Rd., Summer: Daily 10:00 - 5:30, 315-337-0021, Kids (under 15) less than $1

STATEN ISLAND

RICHMONDTOWN (17th to 19th-century restoration, outbuildings, museum, antiques, costumed guides), Arthur Kill Rd., Summer: Daily 10:00 - 5:00, Weekends 2:00 - 5:00 (closed Monday), 212-351-1611, Kids (under 6) free

STATEN ISLAND ZOO (animals, birds & reptiles, aquarium, petting area, kiddie rides), Barrett Park, 614 Broadway, Daily 10:00 - 4:00, 212-442-3101, Under $1

SYRACUSE

BURNETT PARK ZOO (animals, birds, kiddie land), Avery Ave., Summer: Daily 10:00 - 6:00, 315-473-4393, Under $1

UTICA
UTICA ZOO (animals, birds, baby animals, petting area, picnicking),
Steele Hill Rd., Daily 10:00 - 5:00 (Children's zoo Summer only 11:00 -
5:00, Under $1)

NORTH CAROLINA

ASHEBORO
NORTH CAROLINA ZOOLOGICAL PARK (baby animals, petting area,
picnicking), US 220, Daily 9:00 - 5:00, 919-625-1290, Kids (under 12) free

ASHEVILLE
THOMAS WOLFE HOUSE (author's boyhood home, period furnishings),
48 Spruce St., Daily 9:00 - 5:00, Sunday 1:00 - 5:00 (closed Monday), 704-
253-8304, Kids under $1

CHEROKEE
CHEROKEE INDIAN MUSEUM (regional artifacts, multimedia show,
Cherokee crafts), US 441, Summer: Daily 9:00 - 7:00, 704-497-3481, Kids
(under 6) free

DURHAM
NORTH CAROLINA MUSEUM OF LIFE & SCIENCE (natural history
museum, prehistoric animal models, regional items), 433 Murray Ave.,
Daily 10:00 - 5:00, Sunday 2:00 - 5:00 (closed Monday), 919-477-0431,
Kids under $1

GREENSBORO
THE NATURAL SCIENCE CENTER OF GREENSBORO (aquarium, re-
gional wildlife exhibits, planetarium, baby animals, petting area), 4301
Lawndale Dr., 919-288-3769, Daily 9:00 - 5:00, Weekends 2:00 - 5:00,
Under $1, Additional fee (under $2) charged for planetarium show

NEW BERN
FIREMEN'S MUSEUM (old-time firefighting exhibit, memorabilia), 420
Broad St., Daily 9:30 - 4:00, Sunday 1:30 - 4:00 (closed Monday), 919-
638-6010, Under $1
TRYON PALACE & GARDENS (late 18th-century restored colonial estate,
period furnishings, English gardens, costumed tour guides), 613 Pollock
St., Daily 9:30 - 4:00, Sunday 1:30 - 4:00 (closed Monday), 919-638-5109

PINEHURST
WORLD GOLF HALL OF FAME (history of golf exhibits), Ford Blvd.,
Daily 9:00 - 5:00, Kids (under 12) less than $1

RALEIGH
NORTH CAROLINA MUSEUM OF ART (painting & sculpture collection,
art gallery for the blind), 107 E. Morgan St., Daily 10:00 - 5:00, Sunday
2:00 - 6:00 (closed Monday), 919-733-7568, By donation

REIDSVILLE
CHINQUA-PENN PLANTATION (historic home, period furnishings, art
collection, picnicking), US 29, Wentworth Rd., Summer: Daily 10:00 - 4:00,
Sunday 1:00 - 4:00 (closed Monday & Tuesday), 919-349-4576

WILMINGTON
BLOCKADE RUNNER MUSEUM (Civil War dioramas, model ships,
marine memorabilia), US 421 S., Summer: Daily 9:00 - 5:00, Kids (under
6) free

BURGWIN-WRIGHT HOUSE (18th-century historic home, colonial items, garden), 224 Market St., Daily 10:00 - 5:00 (closed Monday), 919-762-0570, Kids under $1

GREENFIELD GARDENS & ZOO (sunken gardens, Venus Fly Trap habitat, zoo, petting area, train ride, picnicking), US 421, Summer: Daily 10:00 - 6:00, 919-763-9871, Under $1

USS NORTH CAROLINA (Battleship Memorial, WW II "Battlewagon," tours), berthed in Cape-Fear River, Summer only: Daily 8:00 - sunset, 919-762-1829, Kids (under 6) free

WINSTON - SALEM

REYNOLDA HOUSE & GARDENS (Southern estate, art collection, extensive gardens, conservatory, trails), Hwy. 67, Daily 9:30 - 4:30, 919-725-5325

NORTH DAKOTA

ABERCROMBIE
FORT ABERCROMBIE STATE HISTORIC SITE (North Dakota's first federal fort, guardhouse, stockade, museum, picnicking), US 81, Summer: Daily 8:00 - 7:00, 701-553-8513, Under $1

BISMARCK
DAKOTA ZOO (regional & domestic animals, bird exhibits, train ride), Sertoma-Riverside Park, Summer: Daily 10:00 - 8:00, 701-223-7543, Kids under $1

FARGO
BONANZAVILLE, U.S.A. (reconstructed pioneer village, museum, log cabins, blacksmith shop, church, train depot, antique autos), US 10, 52, Summer: Daily 9:30 - 5:00, Weekends 1:00 - 5:00, 701-282-2822, Kids (under 6) free

KENMARE
LAKE COUNTRY PIONEER VILLAGE (restored buildings, church, school, history museum), US 52, Summer: Daily 2:00 - 4:00, Kids under $1

MANDAN
FORT LINCOLN HISTORIC STATE PARK (reconstructed blockhouses, Indian earth lodges, regional artifacts museum), Hwy. 1806, Summer: Daily 8:00 - 8:00, 701-633-3049, Vehicle use fee charged

MEDORA
DE MORES CHATEAU & HISTORIC SITE (26 room chateau, authentic furnishings, interpretive center, ruins, guided tours, picnicking), US 10, Summer: Daily 8:30 - 4:30 (tours), 701-623-4355, Under $1

THEODORE ROOSEVELT NATIONAL MEMORIAL PARK (over 70,000 acres, scenic Badlands along Little Missouri River, buffalo herd, visitor center, picnicking), I-94, Summer: Daily 8:00 - 8:00, 701-623-4466, Vehicle use fee charged

WILLISTON
FORT BUFORD STATE HISTORIC SITE (site of Chief Sitting Bull's surrender, powderhouse, museum, picnicking), US 2 W. (look for signs), Summer: Daily 9:00 - 5:00, 701-572-9034, Under $1

FRONTIER MUSEUM (Indian & pioneer artifacts), US 2, 85, Summer: Daily 1:00 - 5:00 (closed Saturday), 701-572-2363, Kids (under 12) free

OHIO

AKRON
AKRON CHILDREN'S ZOO (baby animals, petting & feeding areas, picnicking), 500 Edgewood Ave., Summer: Daily 10:00 - 5:00, 216-375-2298, Under $1

BATH (Akron)
HALE HOMESTEAD & VILLAGE (pioneer buildings, museum, train ride, picnicking), 2686 Oak Hill Rd., Summer: Daily 10:00 - 5:00, Weekends 12:00 - 5:00, 216-666-3711, Kids (under 6) free

CANTON
MOTHER GOOSE LAND (kiddie rides, petting area), US 30, Summer only: Daily 12:00 - 8:00 (closed Monday), 216-454-6969, Under $1
PRO FOOTBALL HALL OF FAME (exhibits, memorabilia, film), I-77 (Exit Fulton Rd.), Summer: Daily 9:00 - 8:00, 216-456-8207, Kids (under 14) less than $1
STARK COUNTY HISTORICAL CENTER (Historical Museum, Hall of Science, planetarium), Monument Park, 749 Hazlett Ave., N.W., Daily 10:00 - 5:00, Weekends 1:30 - 5:00, 216-455-7043, Kids under $1

CHILLICOTHE
ADENA (early 19th-century plantation style mansion, furnishings, outbuildings, gardens), Hwy. 104, Summer: Daily 10:00 - 6:00 (closed Monday), 614-772-1500, Kids (under 12) free
ROSS COUNTY HISTORICAL SOCIETY MUSEUM (regional & local items, pioneer relics, tours), 45 W. 5th St., Summer: Daily 1:00 - 4:00 (closed Monday), 614-772-1936, Kids (under 12) free

CINCINNATI
CAREW TOWER OBSERVATORY (Cincinnati's tallest building), Vine St., Summer: Daily 9:00 - 5:00, Under $1
CINCINNATI ART MUSEUM (painting, sculpture, 18th & 19th-century period rooms), US 22 (Eden Park), Summer: Daily 10:00 - 5:00, Sunday 1:00 - 5:00, 513-721-5204, Kids (under 12) free
CINCINNATI MUSEUM OF NATURAL HISTORY (regional wildlife exhibits, The Cavern scene features a waterfall, Indian collection), 1720 Gilbert Ave. (Eden Park), Summer: Daily 9:00 - 4:30 (closed Monday), 513-621-3889, Under $1

CLEVELAND
CLEVELAND AQUARIUM (marine life exhibits), Gordon Park, 72nd St., Summer: Daily 10:00 - 5:00, 216-391-1527, Under $1
CLEVELAND METROPARKS ZOO (baby animals, feeding & petting areas, kiddie rides), Brookside Park, Summer: Daily 10:00 - 7:00, 216-661-6500, Kids (under 6) free
CLEVELAND MUSEUM OF NATURAL HISTORY (regional exhibits, dinosaur, birds, mammals, precious stones), Wade Oval, University Circle, Daily 10:00 - 5:00, Sunday 1:00 - 5:00, 216-231-4600, Kids (under 6) free
WESTERN RESERVE HISTORICAL SOCIETY & CRAWFORD AUTO-AVIATION MUSEUM (Americana & Indian exhibits, antique autos, aircraft, tours), 10825 E. Boulevard, Daily 10:00 - 5:00, Sunday 12:00 - 6:00 (closed Monday), 216-721-5722, Kids under $1

COLUMBUS
COLUMBUS ZOO (animals, birds, reptiles, kiddie zoo, picnicking), Riverside Park, Rt. 257, Summer: Daily 10:00 - 6:00, 614-887-9471, Kids under $1

OHIO VILLAGE (early 19th-century country village, general store, town hall, blacksmith, period craftsmen), I-71 & 17th Ave., Summer: Daily 10:00 - 6:00 (closed Monday & Tuesday), Kids (under 13) free

DAYTON
AULLWOOD AUDUBON CENTER (self-guiding nature trails, museum, displays), 1000 Aullwood Rd., Hwy. 40 (Englewood Dam), Summer: Daily 7:00 - 8:00 (closed Sunday), 513-890-7336, Kids under $1
DAYTON MUSEUM OF NATURAL HISTORY (natural history scenes, planetarium), 2629 Ridge Ave., Summer: Daily 9:00 - 6:00 (Sunday 2:00 - 6:00), 513-275-7431, Kids under $1
DUNBAR HOUSE (home of black poet, writer Paul Laurence Dunbar), 219 Summit St., Summer: Daily 10:00 - 5:00, Sunday 1:00 - 5:00 (closed Monday & Tuesday), 513-224-7061, Under $1

FREMONT
HAYES MEMORIAL (includes Spiegel Grove, President Hayes' Estate, museum), 1337 Hayes Ave., Daily 9:00 - 5:00, Sunday 1:30 - 5:00, 419-332-2081, Kids (under 13) free

LEBANON
FORT ANCIENT STATE MEMORIAL (100 acre prehistoric earthworks, burial mounds, museum, picnicking), 513-932-4421, Rt. 350, Summer: Daily, Under $1

MASSILLON
SPRING HILL (turn-of-the-century preserved home, outbuildings, picnicking), Rt. 241, Seasonal, 216-833-4061, Kids (under 6) free

MENTOR
HOLDEN ARBORETUM (nature trails, botanical gardens, picnicking), 9500 Sperry Rd., Summer: Daily 10:00 - 7:00 (closed Monday), 216-946-4400, Kids (under 6) free

NEW PHILADELPHIA
SCHOENBRUNN VILLAGE (scene of Ohio's 1st villages, reconstructed buildings, historic museum, picnicking), US 250, Summer: Daily 10:00 - 6:00, 216-343-9711, Kids (under 12) free

TOLEDO
TOLEDO ZOO (over 2,000 animals, birds & reptiles, children's zoo, kiddie rides, picnicking), US 24, Summer: Daily 10:00 - 4:00, 419-385-5721, Kids under $1

VERMILION
GREAT LAKES HISTORICAL SOCIETY MUSEUM (ship models, marine memorabilia), 480 Main St., Summer: Daily 10:00 - 6:00, 216-967-3467, Kids (under 6) free

WAPAKONETA
NEIL ARMSTRONG MUSEUM (history of aviation museum, Gemini 8 space capsule), I-75 & Fisher Rd., Daily 9:30 - 5:00, Sunday 11:00 - 5:00, 419-738-8811, Kids (under 12) free

OKLAHOMA

ELK CITY
OLD TOWN MUSEUM (restoration site, late 19th-century gingerbread frame house, one-room schoolhouse, Old-West doctor's office, outbuildings, period furnishings), US 66, Summer: Daily 10:00 - 8:00, Sunday 2:00 - 5:00 (closed Monday), 405-225-2207, Kids (under 6) free

FREEDOM
ALABASTER CAVERNS STATE PARK (guided tours), Rt. 50, Daily
8:00 - 5:00, 405-621-3391, Kids (under 11) less than $1

MUSKOGEE
ANTIQUE CAR MUSEUM (automobile & airplane collection, picnicking),
2215 W. Shawnee Ave., Summer: Daily 10:00 - 6:00, 918-687-4447, Kids
(under 6) free
FIVE CIVILIZED TRIBES INDIAN MUSEUM (art collection, regional
items), Honor Heights Park (Agency Hill), Daily 10:00 - 5:00, Sunday
1:00 - 5:00, 918-683-1701, Under $1

OKLAHOMA CITY
NATIONAL COWBOY HALL OF FAME (extensive Western art collection, gardens), 1700 N.E. 63rd St., Summer: Daily 8:30 - 6:00, 405-478-
2250, Kids (under 6) free
NATIONAL SOFTBALL HALL OF FAME (history of softball exhibits),
2801 N.E. 50th St., Daily 9:00 - 5:00, Weekends 12:00 - 5:00, 405-424-
5266, Under $1
OKLAHOMA CITY ZOO (children's zoo, picnicking), N.E. 50th St. at
Eastern Ave., Summer: Daily 9:00 - 6:00, 405-424-3344, Kids under $1
OKLAHOMA HERITAGE CENTER (historic house museum), 201 N.W.
14th St., Daily 9:00 - 5:00, Sunday 1:00 - 5:00, 405-235-4458, Kids under $1
OKLAHOMA STATE FIREFIGHTING MUSEUM (Early-West fire equip-
ment), Daily 10:00 - 5:00, 405-424-3440, Kids (under 6) free

PONCA CITY
PONCA CITY CULTURAL CENTER & INDIAN MUSEUM (Indian arts
& crafts, costumes), 1000 E. Grand, Daily 9:00 - 4:00, Sunday 1:00 - 4:00
(closed Monday), 405-765-6123, Kids (under 6) free

TAHLEQUAH
TSA-LA-GI (re-created Cherokee Indian village, costumed Indians, museum), US 62, Summer: Daily 10:00 - 5:00, (closed Monday), 918-456-
6007, Kids (under 16) less than $1

TULSA
PHILBROOK ART CENTER (American Indian art collection, period
rooms), 2727 S. Rockford Rd., Daily 10:00 - 5:00, Sunday 1:00 - 5:00, 918-
749-7941, Kids (under 15) free
TULSA ZOO (baby animals, petting area, train ride, picnicking), Mohawk
Park, US 169, Daily 10:00 - 7:00, 918-835-8471, Under $1

OREGON

ASTORIA
CLATSOP COUNTRY HISTORICAL MUSEUM (local & regional arti-
facts), 441 8th St., Summer: Daily 10:00 - 5:00, 503-325-2203, Under $1
COLUMBIA RIVER MARITIME MUSEUM (maritime history exhibits,
nautical items, includes the lightship Columbia), Exchange & 16th St.,
Summer: Daily 10:30 - 5:00, 503-325-2323, Under $1

CAVE JUNCTION
WOODLAND DEER PARK (domestic animals, buffalos, petting area), US
199 S., Summer: Daily 8:00 - 8:00, 503-592-3802, Kids (under 11) less
than $1

CRATER LAKE
CRATER LAKE NATIONAL PARK (lake of unique blue color in heart of once-active volcano, encircled by multicolored lava walls, visitor center, picnicking), Rt. 62, Summer: Daily, 503-594-2211, Vehicle use fee charged

GOLD HILL
THE HOUSE OF MYSTERY - THE OREGON VORTEX ANTI-GRAVITY HOUSE (anti-gravity phenomenon), Rt. 234, Sardine Creek Rd., Summer: Daily 9:00 - 5:00, 503-855-1543

JACKSONVILLE
PIONEER VILLAGE (historic pioneer outbuildings, horse drawn farm equipment, wagons), Rt. 238, Summer: Daily 9:00 - 8:00, 503-899-1683, Kids under $1

NEWPORT
ROYAL PACIFIC WAX MUSEUM (Josephine Tussaud wax figures, horror & fairyland scenes), 550 S.W. Coast Hwy., Summer: Daily 9:00 - 9:00, 503-265-2062, Kids (under 6) free
THE SCHOONER SARA (old time two-masted sailing ship, exhibits, museum), US 101, S.W. Bay Blvd., Summer: Daily, 11:00 - 8:00, Kids (under 6) free

OREGON CAVES
OREGON CAVES NATIONAL MONUMENT (limestone cavern containing formations of great variety & beauty, guided tours), US 199, Rt. 46 (Cave Junction), 503-476-2534, Summer: Daily 8:00 - 7:00

OREGON CITY
MC LOUGHLIN HOUSE NATIONAL HISTORIC SITE (mid 19th-century home of Dr. John McLoughlin, period furnishings), McLoughlin Park, Summer: Daily 10:00 - 5:00 (closed Mondays), 503-656-5146, Kids under $1

PORTLAND
OREGON MUSEUM OF SCIENCE & INDUSTRY (science exhibits, planetarium), 4015 S.W. Canyon Rd., Summer: Daily 9:00 - 6:00, 503-248-5900, Kids (under 5) free.
PITTOCK MANSION (French Renaissance style architecture), Pittock Acres Park, Summer: Daily, 503-248-4469, Kids under $1
PORTLAND ART MUSEUM (paintings, sculpture), 1219 S.W. Park Ave., Daily 12:00 - 5:00 (closed Monday), 503-226-2811, By donation
WASHINGTON PARK ZOO (baby animals, petting area, picnicking), 4001 S.W. Canyon Rd., Daily 10:00 - sunset, 503-266-1561, Kids (under 6) free

PORT ORFORD
PREHISTORIC GARDENS (life-size prehistoric animals), US 101 S., Daily sunrise - sunset, 503-332-4463

SALEM
BUSH HOUSE (late 1800's historic house museum, authentic items, picnicking), Bush Park, Summer: Daily 12:00 - 5:00, Sunday 2:00 - 5:00, 503-363-4714, Kids under $1

SEASIDE
SEASIDE AQUARIUM (regional sea-life exhibits), 200 N. Promenade, Summer: Daily 9:00 - 8:00, 503-738-6211, Kids (under 6) free

PENNSYLVANIA

ALLENTOWN

TREXLER-LEHIGH COUNTY GAME PRESERVE (herds of animals, children's zoo, picnicking), US 309, Summer: Daily 10:00 - 6:00, 215-799-4171, Under $1 (parking fee charged)

BETHLEHEM

HISTORIC BETHLEHEM (1700's industrial area, restored buildings, period furnishings, tours), 516 Main St., Summer: Daily 1:00 - 4:00, (closed Sunday & Monday), 215-868-6311, Kids under $1

CHADDS FORD

BRANDYWINE RIVER MUSEUM (Howard Pyle & Wyeth family paintings, regional art), US 1, Daily 9:30 - 4:30, 215-388-7601, Kids under $1

ERIE

ERIE ZOO (baby animals, petting area, kiddie rides, tours, picnicking), Glenwood Park, Summer: Daily 10:00 - 8:00, 814-864-4091, Kids (under 6) free

PERRY MEMORIAL HOUSE & DICKSON TAVERN (1800's restored tavern, Black-underground-railroad-station, secret passages), French St., Summer: Daily 1:00 - 4:00, 814-459-9393, Under $1

GETTYSBURG

GETTYSBURG NATIONAL MILITARY PARK (site of historic Civil War battle, over 3,500 acres, self-guiding trails, visitor center, picnicking), Hwy. 134, Summer: Daily 8:00 - 9:00 PM, 717-334-1124, Kids (under 11) free

HAMBURG

HAWK MOUNTAIN SANCTUARY (birds-of-prey sanctuary, overlook), Hwy. 895, Summer: Daily 9:00 - 5:00, 215-756-6961, Kids (under 6) free

HERSHEY

HERSHEY MUSEUM OF AMERICAN LIFE (colonial, regional & Indian collection), US 322, 422, Summer: Daily 10:00 - 5:00, 717-534-3439, Kids (under 11) free

HERSHEY ROSE GARDENS & ARBORETUM (over 20 acres of roses & other flowers, tours), Hwy. 39, Daily 8:00 - sunset, 717-534-3062, Kids (under 10) free

KEMPTON

W. K. & S. STEAM RAILROAD (railroad & trolley rides, model trains, Circus Wonderland, museum, picnicking), Hwy. 143, Summer: Daily 1:00 - 5:00, 215-756-6469

LANCASTER

DUTCH WONDERLAND (amusement theme, storybook characters, sea shows, live entertainment, rides, picnicking), US 30, Summer: Daily 10:00 - 6:00, 717-394-6185.

PENNSYLVANIA FARM MUSEUM OF LANDIS VALLEY (regional agriculture collection, antiques, period items, farm equipment, craft demonstrations), Hwy. 272, Daily 9:00 - 4:00, Sunday 12:00 - 4:00, 717-569-0401, Kids (under 12) free

NEW HOPE

DELAWARE CANAL BOAT RIDES (1800's mule-drawn barge trip), Hwy. 32, New St., Summer: Daily (trips: hourly 1:00 - 6:00), 215-862-2842

PHILADELPHIA
AFRO-AMERICAN HISTORICAL MUSEUM, Arch St., Daily 10:00 - 5:00 (closed Monday) Sunday 12:00 - 5:00, 215-574-3675, Kids under $1
AMERICAN SWEDISH HISTORICAL MUSEUM, 1900 Pattison Ave., Daily 10:00 - 4:00, Saturday 1:00 - 4:00 (closed Sunday and Monday), 215-389-1776, Kids (under 6) free
BARTRAM'S GARDEN (historic colonial home & garden), Elmwood Ave., Daily 9:00 - 4:00, 215-729-5281, By donation
EDGAR ALLAN POE HOUSE, 530 N. 7th St., Daily 10:00 - 5:00, Weekends 2:00 - 5:00, Kids (under 12) free
INTERNATIONAL COIN MUSEUM, Market St., Daily 10:00 - 6:00, 215-928-1790, Kids under $1
"MAN FULL OF TROUBLE" TAVERN (colonial items), 127-129 Spruce St., Summer: Daily 1:00 - 4:00 (closed Monday), 215-922-1759, Under $1
MUSEUM OF AMERICAN JEWISH HISTORY, 55 N. 5th St., Daily 10:00 - 5:00 (closed Saturday), 215-923-3811, Kids under $1
PERELMAN ANTIQUE TOY MUSEUM, 270 S. 2nd St., Daily 10:00 - 5:00, 215-922-1070, Kids under $1
PHILADELPHIA MARITIME MUSEUM, 321 Chestnut St., Daily 10:00 - 5:00, Sunday 1:00 - 5:00, 215-925-5439, By donation
PHILADELPHIA MUSEUM OF ART, Franklin Pkwy., Daily 9:00 - 5:00, 215-763-8100, Kids under $1
RODIN MUSEUM, Franklin Pkwy., Daily 9:00 - 5:00, 215-763-8100, By donation

PITTSBURGH
BUHL PLANETARIUM & INSTITUTE OF POPULAR SCIENCE (Zeiss projector, sky shows, science exhibits, tours), Allegheny Square N., Daily 1:00 - 5:00, Saturday 10:00 - 5:00, 412-321-4300, Kids under $1
CARNEGIE INSTITUTE (art collection, natural history museum), 4400 Forbes Ave., Daily 10:00 - 5:00, Sunday 1:00 - 6:00, (closed Monday), 412-622-3313, By suggested (Kids under $1) donation
PITTSBURGH ZOO (over 2,000 animals, birds & reptiles, children's zoo, aquarium, picnicking), Washington Blvd., Summer: Daily 10:00 - 6:00, 412-441-6262, Kids under $1

SHARTLESVILLE
ROADSIDE AMERICA (miniature village exhibit), I-78 (Exit Shartlesville), US 22, Summer: Daily 9:00 - 8:00, 215-488-6529, Kids (under 6) free

STRASBURG
STRASBURG RAILROAD RIDE (depot, 1800's steam train), Hwy. 741, Seasonal, 717-687-7522

YORK
HISTORICAL SOCIETY OF YORK COUNTY MUSEUM (local & regional items, village square scene), 250 E. Market St., Daily 9:00 - 5:00, Sunday 1:00 - 5:00, 717-848-1587, Kids (under 6) free

RHODE ISLAND

BRISTOL
COGGESHALL FARM MUSEUM (early 1600's farm, live animals, rides, picnicking), Colt State Park, Hwy. 114, Seasonal, 401-253-7482, Kids (under 6) free

HAFFENREFFER MUSEUM OF ANTHROPOLOGY (Indian & tribal arts collection), Hwy. 136, Summer: Daily 1:00 - 5:00 (closed Monday), 401-253-8388, Under $1

NEWPORT
BELCOURT CASTLE (costumed guides), Bellevue Ave., Summer: Daily 10:00 - 6:00, 401-846-0669, Kids (under 6) free
THE BREAKERS (Renaissance-style mansion), Ochre Point Ave., Summer: Daily 10:00 - 5:00, 401-847-6543
CHATEAU-SUR-MER (Victorian-style estate), Bellevue Ave., Summer: Daily 10:00 - 5:00, 401-847-0037, Kids (under 6) free
THE ELMS (French-style chateau), Bellevue Ave., Summer: Daily 10:00 - 5:00, 401-847-0478
INTERNATIONAL TENNIS HALL OF FAME (history of tennis exhibits), 194 Bellevue Ave., Summer: Daily 10:00 - 5:00, 401-846-4567, Kids (under 6) free
MARBLE HOUSE (white-columned palace), Bellevue Ave., Summer: Daily 10:00 - 5:00, 401-847-2445
ROSECLIFF (40 room mansion), Bellevue Ave., Summer: Daily 10:00 - 5:00, 401-847-5793

NORTH KINGSTOWN
SOUTH COUNTY MUSEUM (local & regional items, picnicking), Rt. 2, Quaker Lane, Summer: Daily 11:00 - 5:00 (closed Tuesday), 401-295-0498

PAWTUCKET
SLATER MILL STATE HISTORIC SITE (restored 1800's textile mills, exhibits), Roosevelt Ave., Summer: Daily 10:00 - 5:00, Sunday 1:00 - 5:00, 401-725-8638, Kids (under 14) less than $1

PORTSMOUTH
GREEN ANIMALS (sculpture garden, shrubs & trees shaped into animals and other designs), Hwy. 114, Cory's Lane, Summer: Daily 10:00 - 5:00, 401-683-1267, Kids under $1

PROVIDENCE
JOHN BROWN HOUSE (regional house museum, 18th-century art collection, guided tours), 52 Power St., Daily 11:00 - 3:00, Weekends 1:00 - 4:00, (closed Monday), 401-331-8575, Kids under $1

WARWICK
WARWICK MUSEUM (local & regional items), 334 Knight St., Daily 11:00 - 4:00, Sunday 1:00 - 4:00, (closed Monday), 401-737-0010, Kids under $1

SOUTH CAROLINA

BEAUFORT
BEAUFORT ARSENAL MUSEUM (reconstructed arsenal, 16th-century relics, nature room), 701 Craven St., Daily 10:00 - 5:00, Saturday 10:00 - 1:00, (closed Sunday), By donation

CAMDEN
HISTORIC CAMDEN (American revolution period homes, 4 restored buildings, history exhibits, antiques), US 521, Summer: Daily 10:00 - 5:00, Sunday 1:00 - 5:00, (Closed Monday), 803-432-9841, Kids (under 6) free

CHARLESTON
CHARLESTON MUSEUM (regional items, natural history exhibits), 121 Rutledge Ave., Daily 9:00 - 5:00, Sunday 1:00 - 5:00, 803-722-2996, Kids under $1

CHARLES TOWNE LANDING EXHIBITION PARK (underground exhibits, 17th-century trading ketch, animal forest, picnicking), Hwy. 61, Daily 9:00 - 5:00, 803-556-4450, Kids (under 6) free
CONFEDERATE MUSEUM (Civil War guns, swords, portraits, documents), 188 Meeting St., Wednesday & Friday 1:00 - 3:00, Saturday 1:00 - 4:00, 803-723-1541, Under $1
OLD POWDER MAGAZINE (Charleston's oldest public building, historical exhibits), 79 Cumberland St., Summer: Daily 9:30 - 4:00, (closed Weekends), Under $1
OLD SLAVE MART MUSEUM (slave era culture, arts & crafts), 6 Chalmers St., Daily 10:00 - 5:00, Sunday 2:00 - 5:00, 803-722-0079, Kids (under 7) free
PROVOST DUNGEON (Revolutionary War dungeon, 18th-century wax figure scene), Broad St. (Exchange Building), Summer: Daily 10:00 - 2:00, 803-577-0291, Kids under $1

COLUMBIA
RIVERBANKS ZOOLOGICAL PARK (natural habitat exhibits, polar-bear underwater viewing room, tropical rain forest, picnicking), Riverbanks Park, I-26 (Exit Greystone Blvd.), Summer: Daily 9:30 - sunset, 803-779-8717, Kids (under 6) free
WOODROW WILSON'S BOYHOOD HOME (Wilson memorabilia), 1705 Hampton St., Daily 10:00 - 5:00, Sunday 2:00 - 5:00, 803-254-6333, (closed Monday), Kids under $1

FLORENCE
FLORENCE AIR & MISSILE MUSEUM (planes & missile exhibits, F-80-J "Scorpion" jet, ICBM missile), US 301, Summer: Daily (daylight hours) 803-665-5118

GEORGETOWN
HOPSEWEE PLANTATION (1700's rice plantation), US 17 S., Seasonal, 803-546-7891, Kids (under 6) free
RICE MUSEUM (history of Georgetown's rice), US 17, Front St., Summer: Daily 10:00 - 4:00, Sunday 2:00 - 4:00, 803-546-7423, Kids free

GREENVILLE
CLEVELAND PARK ZOO (animals, birds, picnicking), Cleveland Park, Daily 9:00 - 5:00, 803-232-8079, Under $1

MURRELLS INLET (Myrtle Beach)
BROOKGREEN GARDENS (outdoor museum, sculpture, wildlife park, picnicking), US 17, Daily 9:00 - 4:45, 804-237-4657, Kids (under 6) free

ROCK HILL
MUSEUM OF YORK COUNTY (paintings, natural history, planetarium), Hwy. 161, Summer: Daily 9:00 - 5:00, Sunday 1:00 - 5:00, 803-366-4116, Under $1

SPARTANBURG
WALNUT GROVE (1700's plantation manor house, outbuildings, gardens), I-26 (Exit US 21) County Rd. S-42-196, Summer: Daily 11:00 - 5:00, Sunday 2:00 - 5:00, (closed Monday), 803-585-2441, By donation

SOUTH DAKOTA

CUSTER
JEWEL CAVE NATIONAL MONUMENT (caverns, in limestone formation, consists of series of chambers connected by narrow passages, visitor center, tours), US 16, Daily 605-673-2288

DEADWOOD
BROKEN BOOT GOLD MINE (underground guided tour), US 14A, Summer: Daily 8:00 - 6:00, Kids (under 6) free
GHOSTS OF DEADWOOD GULCH WAX MUSEUM (life size historic scenes), 12 Lee St., Summer: Daily 8:00 - 6:00, 605-578-3583, Kids (under 12) free

HOT SPRINGS
WIND CAVE NATIONAL PARK (limestone caverns in scenic Black Hills, cave tours, bison herd, prairie dog towns, visitor center), US 385, Summer: Daily 8:00 - 7:00, 605-727-2311, Kids (under 6) free (cave tours)

INTERIOR
BADLANDS NATIONAL MONUMENT (extraordinary example of erosion, sedimentary deposits contain great numbers of prehistoric animal fossils, visitor center), I-90, US 16A, 605-433-5361, Vehicle use fee charged

KADOKA
BADLANDS PETRIFIED GARDENS (some of Badlands largest petrified logs, dinosaur tracks, fluorescent minerals exhibit, fossil trees & plants), I-90 (Exit 152), Summer: Daily 8:00 - 8:00, 605-837-2448, Kids (under 14) less than $1

KEYSTONE
BIG THUNDER GOLD MINE (old gold mine tour), US 16A, Summer: Daily 7:30 - 7:30, Kids (under 6) free
PARADE OF PRESIDENTS WAX MUSEUM (life size historical settings), US 16 A, Summer: Daily 7:00 - 9:00, 605-666-4455, Kids (under 7) free

LEAD
THE HOMESTAKE MINE (working gold mine, daily tours), US 14A, 85, Summer: Daily 8:00 - 5:00, 605-584-3110, Kids (under 6) free

MURDO
PIONEER AUTO MUSEUM & ANTIQUE TOWN (over 200 antique autos, tractors, farm machinery, horse-drawn vehicles, old Western pioneer town) Jct. US 16, 83 & I-90, Summer: Daily 7:00 - 10:00, 605-669-9120, Kids (under 6) free

RAPID CITY
HORSELESS CARRIAGE MUSEUM (over 100 antique cars & vehicles), US 16, Summer: Daily 8:00 - 8:00, 605-342-2279, Kids (under 6) free

SIOUX FALLS
GREAT PLAINS ZOO (animal & bird exhibits, picnicking), Sherman Park, Summer: Daily 10:00 - 8:00, 605-339-7059, Kids under $1

TENNESSEE

CHATTANOOGA
CONFEDERAMA (multimedia "Battle of Chattanooga"), 3742 Tennessee Ave., Summer: Daily 9:00 - 9:00, Sunday 1:00 - 9:00, 615-821-2812, Kids (under 6) free

HUNTER MUSEUM OF ART (painting, sculpture & graphic art collection), 10 Bluff View, Daily 10:00 - 4:00, Sunday 1:00 - 4:00, (closed Monday), 615-267-0968, By donation
LOOKOUT MOUNTAIN HISTORY MUSEUM (regional items), Lookout Mountain Point Park, Summer: Daily 9:00 - 8:00, Under $1
LOOKOUT MOUNTAIN INCLINE (claimed to be world's steepest passenger railroad), 3917 St. Elmo Ave., Summer: Daily 8:30 - 9:30, 615-821-9056, Kids (under 6) free
TENNESSEE VALLEY RAILROAD MUSEUM (old-time trains, antiques, steam-train ride), 2202 N. Chamberlain Ave., Seasonal, Kids (under 6) **free**

DICKSON
RUSKIN & JEWEL CAVES (cave tours, picnicking), Summer: Daily, 615-383-2887

FRANKLIN
CARTER HOUSE (historic house museum, Civil War exhibits, tours), US 31, Daily 9:00 - 4:00, Sunday 2:00 - 4:00, 615-794-1733, Kids (under 16) less than $1

GATLINBURG
AMERICAN HISTORICAL WAX MUSEUM (historic scenes), US 441, Summer: Daily 8:00 - 11:00 PM, 615-436-4462, Kids (under 6) free
COX'S ANTIQUE CAR MUSEUM (old-time autos), US 441, Summer: Daily 9:00 - 11:00 PM, 615-436-4072, Kids (under 6) free

JACKSON
HOME OF CASEY JONES & THE RAILROAD MUSEUM (folklore character's home, railroad memorabilia, steam engine exhibit), 211 W. Chester St., Daily 9:00 - 4:00, Sunday 1:00 - 4:00, 901-427-8382, Kids (under 6) free

JOHNSON CITY
ROCKY MOUNT (18th-century log cabin, period furnishings, folk art museum), US 11 E., Summer: Daily 10:00 - 5:00, 615-538-7396, Sunday 2:00 - 6:00
TIPTON-HAYNES LIVING HISTORICAL FARM (late 1700's restored farmhouse, outbuildings), US 11, Summer: Daily 10:00 - 5:00, Sunday 2:00 - 6:00, 615-926-3631, Kids under $1

KNOXVILLE
BLOUNT MANSION (18th-century home of Governor William Blount, authentic furnishings, garden), 200 W. Hill Ave., Summer: Daily 9:30 - 5:00, (closed Monday), 615-525-2375, Kids under $1
DULIN GALLERY OF ART (painting, sculpture & graphic arts collection), 3100 Kingston Pike, Daily 1:00 - 5:00, (closed Monday), 615-525-6101, Kids free
KNOXVILLE ZOOLOGICAL PARK (aquarium, animals, birds, reptiles, kiddie rides, petting area, picnicking), 1009 Mary St., Summer: Daily 10:00 - 5:00, 615-637-5331, Kids (under 6) free
MARBLE SPRINGS RESTORATION (farmhouse, barn, outbuildings), US 441 S., Summer: Daily 10:00 - 5:00, Sunday 2:00 - 5:00, 615-573-5508, Under $1
SWAN POND (late 18th-century marble mansion, antiques), Thorngrove Pike, Daily 10:00 - 5:00, Sunday 1:00 - 5:00, (closed Monday), Kids under $1
UNITED DAUGHTERS OF THE CONFEDERACY MEMORIAL HALL (restored antebellum estate, authentic furnishings, antiques, tours), 3148 Kingston Pike, Summer: Daily 2:00 - 5:00, (closed Monday), 615-522-2371, Kids under $1

MEMPHIS
CHUCALISSA MUSEUM (ancient Indian village, archeological exhibits, reconstructed dwellings), US 61, Mitchell Rd., Daily 9:00 - 5:00, Sunday 1:00 - 5:00, (closed Monday), 901-785-3160, Under $1
FONTAINE HOUSE (19th-century restored mansion, antiques), 680 Adams Ave., Daily 1:00 - 4:00, 901-526-1469, Kids under $1
MALLORY-NEELY HOUSE (1800's restored Victorian mansion, authentic furnishings), 652 Adams Ave., Daily 1:00 - 4:00, Kids (under 6) free
MEMPHIS PINK PALACE MUSEUM (natural history museum, regional items), 3050 Central Ave., Daily 9:00 - 5:00, Sunday 1:00 - 5:00, (closed Monday), 901-454-5609, Kids under $1
OVERTON PARK ZOO & AQUARIUM (animal, bird & reptile exhibits, petting area, kiddie rides, picnicking), Overton Park, Summer: Daily 9:00 - 6:00, 901-726-4787, Kids under $1

MURFREESBORO
OAKLANDS (19th-century historic house museum, period rooms, antiques, garden), Maney Ave., Daily 10:00 - 4:00, Sunday 1:00 - 4:00, (closed Monday), 615-893-0022, Kids under $1

NASHVILLE
COUNTRY MUSIC HALL OF FAME & MUSEUM (history of country music exhibits, memorabilia), 4 Music Square E., Summer: Daily 8:00 - 8:00 P.M., 615-244-2522, Kids (under 5) free
CUMBERLAND MUSEUM & SCIENCE CENTER (science exhibits, planetarium, live animals), 800 Ridley Ave., Daily 10:00 - 5:00, Sunday 1:00 - 5:00, (closed Monday), 615-242-1858, Kids under $1
TENNESSEE BOTANICAL GARDENS & FINE ARTS CENTER (painting & sculpture collection, formal gardens, conservatory, boxwood garden), Hwy. 100, Cheek Rd. (Cheekwood), Daily 10:00 - 5:00, Sunday 1:00 - 5:00, (closed Monday), 615-352-5310, Kids under $1
TRAVELLERS' REST (historic house museum, period furnishings, regional items), US 31, Farrell Pkwy., Daily 9:00 - 4:00, Sunday 1:00 - 4:00, 615-832-2962, Kids under $1

NORRIS
MUSEUM OF APPALACHIA (restored area, outbuildings, pioneer cabins, blacksmith shop), Hwy. 61, Daily 8:00 - 8:00, 615-494-7680, Kids (under 6) free

TEXAS

ABILENE
ABILENE ZOO (animals, birds, kiddie rides, picnicking), Nelson Park, Summer: Daily 10:00 - 7:00, 915-672-9771, Kids under $1

AUSTIN
DAUGHTERS OF THE REPUBLIC & TEXAS CONFEDERATE MUSEUM (pioneer & Civil War items), 112 E. 11th St., Seasonal, 512-477-1822, By donation
OLD FRENCH LEGATION (19th-century restored building, period furnishings), 802 San Marcos St., Daily 1:00 - 5:00, (closed Monday), 512-472-8180, Kids under $1

BEAUMONT
SPINDLETOP BOOMTOWN (reconstructed oil town, outbuildings, antiques, period furnishings), US 69, 287, Daily 1:00 - 5:00, 713-838-8122, Under $1

BROWNSVILLE
GLADYS PORTER ZOO (natural habitat exhibits, baby animals, petting area), 500 Ringgold, St., Daily 10:00 - 7:00, 512-546-7187, Kids (under 12) less than $1

CORSICANA
PIONEER VILLAGE (Old-West buildings, period furnishings, historical exhibits, blacksmith), 912 W. Park Ave., Daily 9:00 - 5:00, Sunday 1:00 - 5:00, 214-872-1468, Under $1 (Kids under 6 free)

DALLAS
AGE OF STEAM MUSEUM (railroad equipment & memorabilia, picnicking), State Fair Park, Sunday 12:00 - 5:00, 214-823-9931, Kids under $1
DALLAS ZOO (animals, birds reptiles, aquarium, petting area, train ride), Marsalis Park, Summer: Daily 9:00 - 6:00, 214-946-5155, Under $1 (Kids under 11 free)
OLD CITY PARK RESTORATION (turn-of-the-century Dallas, outbuildings, period furnishings, pioneer relics, antiques, historic museum), St. Paul St., Daily 10:00 - 4:00, Weekends 2:00 - 4:00 214-421-5141, Kids under $1

FORT WORTH
FOREST PARK'S PIONEER VILLAGE (Early-West buildings, log cabins), Forest Park, US 89, Daily 8:00 - 4:00, Weekends 1:00 - 4:00, 817-926-5881, Under $1
FORT WORTH ZOO (animals, birds, reptiles, aquarium, children's zoo), Forest Park, Daily 9:00 - 5:30, 817-923-4637, Kids (under 12) free

GALVESTON
ASHTON VILLA (turn-of-the-century estate, authentic items, carriage-house, tours), 2328 B'way, Summer: Daily 10:00 - 4:00, Weekends 1:00 - 5:00, 713-762-3933, Kids under $1
BISHOP'S PALACE (19th-century mansion, antiques, art collection, tours), 1402 B'way, Summer: Daily 10:00 - 5:00, 713-762-2475, Kids under $1

HUNTSVILLE
SAM HOUSTON HOUSE (historic house museum, Houston memorabilia, pioneer relics, outbuildings, picnicking), US 190, 1804 Sam Houston Ave., Daily 9:00 - 5:00, 713-295-7824, By donation

ROCKWALL (Dallas)
CHAPMAN AUTO MUSEUM (old-time autos), I-30 (Exit Rockwall), Daily 10:00 - 6:00, Sunday 12:00 - 6:00, Kids (under 6) free

SAN ANTONIO
BRACKENRIDGE PARK ART & SCIENCE MUSEUM (Witte Memorial, natural science exhibits, pioneer buildings), US 81, Summer: Daily 9:30 - 6:30, 512-826-0647, Kids under $1
BRACKENRIDGE PARK TEXAS RANGER MUSEUM (Ranger history exhibits, pioneer relics), US 81, Daily 11:00 - 4:00, (closed Monday), Kids (under 6) free
BRACKENRIDGE PARK ZOO (animal shows, aquarium, petting area, train ride, picnicking), US 81, Summer: Daily 9:30 - 6:30, 512-734-7183, Kids under $1
JOSE ANTONIO NAVARRO SITE (historic homes, preserved adobes, authentic items, tours), 228-232 S. Laredo St., Daily 10:00 - 4:00, 512-226-4801, Under $1 (Kids under 6 free)
LONE STAR HALL OF TEXAS HISTORY WAX MUSEUM (historical scenes), Hemisfair Plaza Way, Daily 10:00 - 6:00, 512-226-8301, Kids (under 6) free

MUSEUM OF TRANSPORTATION (old-time vehicles), Hemisfair Plaza Way, Daily 10:00 - 6:00, 512-226-1201, Under $1

"REMEMBER THE ALAMO" THEATRE & MUSEUM (multimedia show, historical museum) 315 Alamo Plaza, Daily 9:00 - 5:30, 512-224-1836, Kids (under 12) less than $1

STEVE'S HOMESTEAD (19th-century estate, period items, outbuildings, garden), 509 King William St., Daily 1:00 - 5:00, Kids under $1

TOWER OF THE AMERICAS OBSERVATION DECK, Hemisfair Plaza Way, Daily, Kids under $1

WACO

TEXAS RANGER HALL OF FAME (Ranger history scenes, film), Fort Fisher Park, Daily 9:00 - 6:00, Sunday 12:00 - 6:00, 817-756-2211, Kids (under 6) free

UTAH

BRYCE CANYON

BRYCE CANYON NATIONAL PARK (some of the most colorful & unusual erosional forms in the world, visitor center, exhibits, picnicking), US 89, Hwy. 12 (Panguitch), Summer: Daily 8:00 - 7:00, 801-834-5322, Vehicle use fee charged

CORINNE

RAILROAD VILLAGE (old fashioned trains, railroad depot, antiques, museum), Rt. 83, Summer: Daily 9:00 - 5:00, Sunday 2:00 - 5:00, Under $1

LOGAN

MAN AND HIS BREAD MUSEUM (history of agriculture exhibits, farming items), Utah State University, US 89, 91, Summer: Daily 10:00 - 4:00, 801-752-4100, Kids (under 12) less than $1

MOAB

ARCHES NATIONAL PARK (erosional arches, windows, pinnacles, & pedestals, visitor center, picnicking), US 163, Summer: Daily 8:00 - 6:00

NATURAL BRIDGES

NATURAL BRIDGES NATIONAL MONUMENT (three natural bridges carved out of sandstone, visitor center, Indian ruins, picnicking), Rt. 95 (Blanding), Summer: Daily 8:00 - 5:00

SALT LAKE CITY

HANSEN PLANETARIUM (changing shows, science exhibits, museum), 16 S. State St., Daily, 801-364-3611, Kids (under 12) less than $1

HOGLE ZOOLOGICAL GARDENS (natural habitat exhibits, baby animals, petting area, kiddie rides, picnicking), 2600 Sunnyside Ave., Summer: Daily 9:30 - 6:00, 801-582-1631, Kids (under 15) less than $1

UTAH MUSEUM OF NATURAL HISTORY (natural science displays, regional exhibits), University of Utah, Daily 9:30 - 5:30, 801-581-6927, Kids under $1

SPRINGDALE

ZION NATIONAL PARK (colorful canyon & mesa scenery, former volcanic activity, visitor center, museum, picnicking), Rt. 15, Daily 8:00 - 5:00, 801-772-3256, Kids (under 16) free

TIMPANOGOS CAVE

TIMPANOGOS CAVE NATIONAL MONUMENT (limestone cavern located on north side of Mt. Timpanogos, guided tours, visitor center, picnicking), Rt. 80 (American Fork), Summer: Daily 8:00 - 5:00, 801-756-4497, Kids (under 15) free

VERMONT

BARRE (Graniteville)
ROCK OF AGES (guided quarry tours, craftsman center, visitor center, overlook), Rt. 14, Summer: Daily 8:30 - 5:00, (craftsman center: Daily 8:30 - 3:30), 802-476-3115, Free (fee charged for quarry train ride)

BENNINGTON
BENNINGTON BATTLE MONUMENT (late 19th-century 306 feet high monument, observation tower), Monument Ave., Summer: Daily 9:00 - 6:00, 802-828-3226, Under $1
BENNINGTON MUSEUM (regional items, Grandma Moses collection), West Main St., Summer: Daily 9:00 - 6:00, 802-442-2180, Kids (under 12) free
OLD FIRST CHURCH (early 19th-century restored church, graveyard, tours), Monument Ave., Summer: Daily 10:00 - 5:00, Sunday 1:00 - 5:00, By donation

MANCHESTER
SOUTHERN VERMONT ART CENTER (local & regional exhibits), US 7, Summer: Daily 10:00 - 5:00, Sunday 1:00 - 5:00, (closed Monday), 802-362-1405, Kids (under 12) free

MIDDLEBURY
SHELDON MUSEUM (historical house museum, period furnishings, Old Country Store), Park St., Summer: Daily 10:00 - 5:00 (closed Sunday), 802-388-2117, Kids under $1

NEWPORT (Brownington)
OLD STONE HOUSE MUSEUM (regional & antique items), US 5, Summer: Daily 9:00 - 5:00, 802-754-2022, Kids under $1

PLYMOUTH
COOLIDGE HOMESTEAD (President Coolidge's boyhood home, museum), Rt. 100A, Summer: Daily 9:30 - 5:30, 802-828-3226, Kids (under 13) free

ST. JOHNSBURY
MAPLE GROVE MUSEUM (exhibits, candy factory tour, film), US 2, Summer: Daily 9:00 - 5:00, (last tour at 4:30), 802-985-3344, Under $1 (Kids under 12 free)

SPRINGFIELD
EUREKA SCHOOLHOUSE (18th-century restored schoolhouse), Charleston Rd., Summer: Daily 10:00 - 5:00, 802-885-3035, By donation

WESTON
FARRAR-MANSUR HOUSE (18th-century restored tavern), Rt. 100, Summer: Daily 1:00 - 5:00, 802-824-5884, Under $1 (kids under 11 free)

VIRGINIA

ALEXANDRIA
ROBERT E. LEE HOUSE (General Lee's boyhood home, period furnishings), 607 Oronoco St., Summer: Daily 10:00 - 4:00, Sunday 12:00 - 4:00, 703-548-8454, Kids (under 6) free

APPOMATTOX
APPOMATTOX COURT HOUSE NATIONAL HISTORICAL PARK (scene of surrender of the Confederate Army, restored village, visitor center, self-guided tours), Hwy. 24, Summer: Daily 8:30 - 6:00, 804-352-8987, Vehicle use fee charged

ARLINGTON
ARLINGTON NATIONAL CEMETERY GUIDED TOUR (historical memorials: Arlington House, Confederate Memorial, Grave of Pres. John F. Kennedy, Marine Corps War Memorial, Tomb of the Unknown Soldier), Arlington Ridge Rd. (Visitor Center), Summer: Daily 8:00 - 6:00, 703-545-6700, Kids under $1

CHARLES CITY
BERKELEY PLANTATION (early 18th-century Southern plantation, antiques, boxwood gardens), Hwy. 5, Daily 8:00 - 5:00, 703-829-2445, Kids (under 6) free

CHARLOTTESVILLE
HISTORIC MICHIE TAVERN MUSEUM (period furnishings, antiques, tours, outbuildings), Hwy. 53, Daily 9:00 - 5:00, 804-973-5842, Kids (under 6) free
MONTICELLO (Thomas Jefferson's historic mansion, restored, garden), Hwy. 53, Summer: Daily 8:00 - 5:00, 804-295-2657, Kids under $1

FREDERICKSBURG
JAMES MONROE MUSEUM (Mr. Monroe's law office, memorabilia), 908 Charles St., Daily 9:00 - 5:00, 703-373-8426, Kids under $1
KENMORE (18th-century restored colonial estate, period furnishings, gardens), 1201 Washington Ave., Summer: Daily 9:00 - 5:00, 703-373-3381, Kids (under 6) free
MARY WASHINGTON HOUSE (George Washington's mother's home, English garden), 1200 Charles St., Summer: Daily 9:00 - 5:00, 703-371-1569, Kids (under 6) free
RISING SUN TAVERN (1700's restored tavern, exhibits), 1306 Caroline St., Summer: Daily 9:00 - 5:00, 703-371-1494, Kids (under 6) free

JAMESTOWN
COLONIAL NATIONAL HISTORICAL PARK (site of 1st permanent English settlement in America, ruins, self-guided tours, visitor center, films, picnicking), Colonial Pkwy., Summer: Daily 8:00 - 5:00, 804-229-3107, Vehicle use fee charged

LORTON
GUNSTON HALL (18th-century plantation, period furnishings, gardens, picnicking), Hwy. 242, 703-550-9220, Kids (under 16) less than $1

MOUNT VERNON
MOUNT VERNON (George Washington's estate, memorabilia, original furnishings, outbuildings), Mt. Vernon Memorial Hwy., Summer: Daily 9:00 - 5:00, 703-780-2000, Kids (under 6) free

NEWPORT NEWS
MARINERS MUSEUM (famous ship models, extensive marine collection), US 60, Daily 9:00 - 5:00, Sunday 12:00 - 5:00, 804-595-0368, Kids under $1
PENINSULA NATURE AND SCIENCE CENTER (planetarium, aquarium, live animals), Deer Park, Daily 10:00 - 5:00, Sunday 1:00 - 5:00, 804-595-1900, Under $1

NORFOLK
CHRYSLER MUSEUM (painting, sculpture & glassware collection), Olney Rd., Daily 10:00 - 5:00, Sunday 1:00 - 5:00 (closed Monday), 804-622-1211, By suggested (under $1.50) donation
NORFOLK BOTANICAL GARDENS - GARDENS-BY-THE-SEA (over 150 acres, observation tower, tours, picnicking), Azalea Garden Rd., Airport Ave., Daily 8:00 - sunset, 804-855-0195, Under $1

RICHMOND
VALENTINE MUSEUM (local & regional history, period costumes, Indian items), 1015 E. Clay St., Daily 10:00 - 4:45, Sunday 1:30 - 5:00, (closed Monday), 804-649-0711, Kids (under 6) free
VIRGINIA HISTORICAL SOCIETY - BATTLE ABBEY (classic Greek structure, history exhibits, paintings), 428 N. Boulevard, Daily 9:00 - 5:00, Weekends 2:00 - 5:00, 804-358-4901, Kids (under 12) free
VIRGINIA MUSEUM OF FINE ARTS (paintings, sculpture & jewelry exhibits), Grove Ave., Daily 11:00 - 5:00, Sunday 1:00 - 5:00, (closed Monday), 804-786-6344, Under $1

SHENANDOAH
SHENANDOAH NATIONAL PARK (outstanding portion of Blue Ridge Mountains, magnificent vistas of Shenandoah Valley, wildlife, picnicking, visitor center), Headquarters: US 211 (Luray), Daily, 703-999-2266, Vehicle use fee charged

STRATFORD
STRATFORD HALL PLANTATION (1700's working plantation, visitor center, museum), Hwy. 214, Daily 9:00 - 4:30, 804-493-3882, Kids under $1

YORKTOWN
YORKTOWN BATTLEFIELD (scene of culminating battle of American Revolution, visitor center, self-guiding tours), Colonial Pkwy., Summer: Daily 8:00 - 6:00, 804-898-3400, Free

WASHINGTON

ABERDEEN-HOQUIAM
HOQUIAM'S CASTLE (19th-century restored 20-room mansion, period furnishings, antiques), 515 Chenault Ave., Summer: Daily 11:00 - 5:00, Kids (under 6) free

GOLDENDALE
MARYHILL MUSEUM OF FINE ARTS (paintings, antiques, Indian artifacts) US 97, Rt. 14 (Maryhill), Summer: Daily 9:00 - 5:00, 509-773-4792, Kids (under 7) free

MOUNT RAINIER
MOUNT RAINIER NATIONAL PARK (greatest single-peak glacial system in the United States, dense forests, flowered meadows, visitor centers, self-guided trails), Rt. 706 (Paradise Visitors Center), Daily, 206-569-2211, Vehicle use fee charged

SEATTLE
NORTHWEST SEAPORT (sailing ships, marine vessels, exhibits), Lake St., Summer: Daily, 206-828-6685, Kids under $1
PACIFIC SCIENCE CENTER (science exhibits, planetarium, films), Seattle Center, Summer: Daily 10:00 - 7:00, 206-624-3724, Kids (under 5) free

PIONEER SQUARE WAX MUSEUM (historical scenes), 112 1st Ave., S., Summer: Daily 9:30 - 9:00, 206-624-6486

SEATTLE ART MUSEUM (famous art collection), Volunteer Park, Daily 10:00 - 5:00, Sunday 12:00 - 5:00, (closed Monday) 206-447-4710, Kids (under 12) free

SEATTLE CENTER SPACE NEEDLE OBSERVATION DECK, Seattle Center, Summer: Daily, 206-682-5656, Kids (under 6) free

SPOKANE

PACIFIC NORTHWEST INDIAN CENTER (Indian collection, paintings, artifacts), E. 200 Cataldo St., Daily 9:00 - 6:00, Sunday 12:00 - 8:00, 509-326-4550, Kids under $1

WENATCHEE

OHME GARDENS (Alpine rock garden, stone pathways, pools, waterfall, lookout), US 97, Ohme Rd., Summer: Daily 8:00 - sunset, 509-662-5785, Kids (under 12) free

YAKIMA

YAKIMA VALLEY HISTORICAL MUSEUM (pioneer & Indian collection), Franklin Park, Daily 10:00 - 5:00, Weekends 12:00 - 5:00, (closed Monday & Tuesday), 509-248-0747, Kids under $1

WEST VIRGINIA

BECKLEY

BECKLEY EXHIBITION COAL MINE (old coal mine tour), New River City Park, Summer: Daily 10:00 - 6:00

BLUEFIELD

SKYLAND ("Ridge-Runner" narrow gauge railroad, 8 minute train ride, Museum of the Hills, regional artifacts), I-77, US 21, 52, Summer: Daily 9:00 - 5:00, 304-456-4300, Under $1

CHARLESTON

SUNRISE CHILDREN'S MUSEUM & PLANETARIUM (art, science & natural history exhibits, includes Garden Center), Myrtle Road, Summer: Daily 10:00 - 4:00, Sunday 2:00 - 5:00, (closed Monday), 304-344-8035, Under $1

DAVIS

MOUNTAIN STATE HISTORICAL MUSEUM (natural, antiques & regional items), William St., Summer: Daily 10:00 - 10:00 (closed Friday), 304-259-5323, Kids (under 6) free

HARPERS FERRY

JOHN BROWN WAX MUSEUM (historical scenes), High St., Summer: Daily 9:00 - 5:00, 304-535-6342, Kids under $1

HILLSBORO

PEARL S. BUCK BIRTHPLACE (historical house museum, exhibits), US 219, Daily 9:00 - 5:00, Sunday 1:00 - 5:00, 304-653-4430, Kids (under 6) free

POINT PLEASANT

POINT PLEASANT BATTLE MONUMENT & MUSEUM (late 18th-century historic house museum, colonial furnishings, antiques), Main St., Summer: Daily 9:00 - 5:00, 304-675-3330, By donation

WHEELING
MANSION HOUSE MUSEUM (antiques, period rooms, regional items), Oglebay Park, Daily 9:30 - 5:00, Sunday 1:30 - 5:00, 304-242-7272, Kids (under 12) free
OGLEBAY PARK ART GALLERY (paintings), Oglebay Park, Rt. 88, 304-242-7272, Free
OGLEBAY PARK ZOO (includes nature center, picnicking), Rt. 88, 304-242-3000, Free
WILLOW GLEN MUSEUM (baronial-style mansion, antiques), Hwy. 88, Seasonal, 304-233-0292, Kids (under 6) free

WISCONSIN

BARABOO
AMERICAN PHOTOGRAPHY MUSEUM (pioneer & contemporary equipment, photography exhibits), 232 Water St., Summer: Daily 10:00 - 7:00, Kids (under 5) free
SAUK COUNTY HISTORICAL SOCIETY MUSEUM (regional, pioneer & Indian items), 531 4th Ave., Summer only: Daily 2:00 - 5:00 (closed Monday), 608-356-6016, Under $1

BOULDER JUNCTION
AQUALAND - WHITE BIRCH FISHERIES (regional wildlife, fishing, petting zoo, picnicking), US 51, US 45, Summer: Daily 9:00 - 5:00, 715-385-2181, Kids (under 4) free

EPHRAIM
ANDERSON MUSEUM (old-time country store, museum), Rt. 42, Summer only: Daily 10:00 - 5:00 (closed Sunday), 414-854-4142, By donation

FOND DU LAC
GALLOWAY HOUSE & VILLAGE (restored mansion, historic outbuildings) 336 Old Pioneer Rd., Summer only: Daily 1:00 - 4:00 (closed Monday), 414-922-6390, Kids (under 5) free

GREEN BAY
HAZELWOOD (early 19th-century historic home), 1008 S. Monroe Ave., Summer: Daily 10:00 - 5:00, Sunday 2:00 - 5:00, (closed Monday), 414-497-3768, Under $1
HERITAGE HILL STATE PARK HISTORIC SITE (restored outbuildings, period furnishings, tours), 2640 S. Webster Ave., Summer: Daily 9:00 - 5:00, 414-497-4368, Kids (under 6) free
NATIONAL RAILROAD MUSEUM (old-time train exhibits, memorabilia, train rides, picnicking), 2285 S. B'way, Summer: Daily 9:00 - 5:00, 414-435-5875, Kids (under 6) free

HAYWARD
NATIONAL FRESH WATER FISHING HALL OF FAME (mounted fish exhibits, memorabilia), Wisconsin Ave., Summer: Daily 10:00 - 5:00, 715-634-4440, Kids under $1

HAZELHURST
WARBONNET ZOO (baby animals, petting & feeding area), US 51, Summer: Daily 9:00 - 6:00, 715-356-5093

KAUKAUNA
GRIGNON (late 18th-century restored home, pioneer & Indian items, picnicking), US 41, Summer only: Daily 9:00 - 5:00 (closed Monday), 414-766-3122, Under $1

MANITOWOC

MANITOWOC MARITIME MUSEUM (marine history exhibits, memorabilia), 809 S. 8th St., Summer: Daily 9:00 - 5:00, 414-684-8381, Kids (under 7) free

U.S.S. COBIA (Submariners Memorial, World War II submarine), South 9th St., Summer: Daily 9:00 - 5:00, Kids (under 7) free

MILWAUKEE

BROOKS STEVENS AUTOMOTIVE MUSEUM (old-time cars, exhibits), US 141 N., (Mequon), Summer: Daily 10:00 - 5:00, 414-241-4185

EXPERIMENTAL AIRCRAFT MUSEUM (almost 100 aircrafts on display, memorabilia), 1311 W. Forest Home Ave., (Franklin), Summer: Daily 9:00 - 5:00, Sunday 11:00 - 5:00, 414-425-4860, Kids (under 6) free

MILWAUKEE COUNTY ZOOLOGICAL PARK (animals, birds & reptiles, petting area, tours), US 18, Daily 10:00 - 5:00, 414-771-3040, Kids under $1 (parking fee charged)

MILWAUKEE PUBLIC MUSEUM (natural history exhibits), 800 W. Wells St., Daily 9:00 - 5:00 (closed Holidays), 414-278-2700, Kids under $1

PRAIRIE DU CHIEN

VILLA LOUIS (historical restoration, period furnishings, regional museum, garden, tours), US 18, Summer only: Daily 9:00 - 5:00 (closed Holidays), 608-326-2721, Kids (under 6) free

WYOMING

CODY

BUFFALO BILL HISTORICAL CENTER (Buffalo Bill memorabilia, Plains Indian Museum, Whitney Gallery of Western Art), US 14, 16, 20, Summer: Daily 7:00 - 10:00, 307-587-4771, Kids under $1

DEVILS TOWER

DEVILS TOWER NATIONAL MONUMENT (our 1st national monument, an 865 ft. tower of columnar rock, the remains of a volcanic intrusion, visitor center, picnicking), US 14, Rt. 24 (Sundance), Summer: Daily 8:00 - 8:00, 307-467-5370, Vehicle use fee charged

GRAND TETON (Moose)

GRAND TETON NATIONAL PARK (series of peaks comprising the most spectacular part of the Teton range, visitor centers, picnicking), US 26, 89, 187, Summer: Daily, 307-733-2880, Vehicle use fee charged

JACKSON

JACKSON HOLE MUSEUM (pioneer & Indian artifacts), 101 N. Glenwood Ave., Summer: Daily 9:00 - 8:00, 307-733-2414, Kids under $1

LARAMIE

LARAMIE PLAINS MUSEUM (early Victorian style mansion, period furnishings, antiques, paintings, carriage-house), US 30, Summer: Daily 9:00 - 5:00 (closed Saturday & Sunday), 307-742-4448, Kids under $1

LUSK

STAGECOACH MUSEUM (Indian & pioneer artifacts, authentic Concord stagecoach), US 85, Summer: Daily 1:00 - 5:00 & 7:00 - 9:00, 307-334-3444, Under $1 (kids under 12 free)

NEWCASTLE

ACCIDENTAL OIL COMPANY (hand dug producing oil well, guided tours), US 16 E., Summer: Daily 8:00 - 8:00, 307-746-2042, Kids (under 6) free

SHERIDAN

TRAIL END HISTORICAL HOME (historic house museum, period furnishings, garden), 400 Clarendon St., Summer: Daily 9:00 - 5:00, Sunday 1:00 - 5:00, 307-674-4589, Kids under $1

YELLOWSTONE

YELLOWSTONE NATIONAL PARK (America's first & largest national park, world's greatest geyser area, with about 3,000 geysers & hot springs, spectacular falls & canyons of the Yellowstone River, wildlife sanctuary, black bears, visitor centers, museum, self-guided trails, picnicking), US 89 (Mammoth Hot Springs, Visitor Center), Seasonal, 307-344-7381, Vehicle use fee charged

PILOT BOOKS TRAVEL GUIDES

NATIONAL DIRECTORY OF BUDGET MOTELS edited by Raymond Carlson. A geographic listing of America's leading low cost chain motels offering overnight accommodations costing generally between $10.00 and $15 for a single occupancy (some are cheaper). These motels meet rigid standards and are outstanding values. They are conveniently located along major highway systems. $2.95

NATIONAL DIRECTORY OF FREE VACATION AND TRAVEL INFORMATION edited by Raymond Carlson. This directory shows you where to obtain free brochures, maps, pamphlets, calendars of events and descriptive travel literature. You can find specific information concerning our states, cities, parks, forests, recreational areas, landmarks and other tourist attractions. Lists over 600 sources that offer free tourist information. $2.95

NATIONAL DIRECTORY OF THEME PARKS AND AMUSEMENT AREAS edited by Raymond Carlson. A state-by-state listing of over 500 Theme Parks, Amusement Parks, Kiddielands and Storybook or Fantasy Lands. These offer a wide range of opportunities for family enjoyment. $2.95

NATIONAL DIRECTORY OF FREE TOURIST ATTRACTIONS edited by Raymond Carlson. Enjoy free gardens, restored villages, ships, museums and other interesting presentations of history, science, folk and fine art throughout the United States. The attractions that are listed will make every one of your trips more enjoyable. $2.95

PAN FOR GOLD ON YOUR NEXT VACATION by Janet Ruhe-Schoen. Try something different on your vacation. Enjoy an exciting, economical unique adventure. Gold country is beautiful and offers a real change-of-pace. The gold you find can help finance your trip—and perhaps even more. This book shows you how and where to—tells you everything you need to get started. $2.50

CURTIS CASEWIT'S GUIDE TO TENNIS RESORTS. Directory for the tennis playing traveler. Know what you're getting into in the way of costs and facilities. Contains up-to-date listings, complete with current telephone numbers and most recent number of courts. A brief description of each resort is given along with the price range. Thirty seven states are listed plus resorts in Canada and Puerto Rico. $2.50

Pilot Books 347 fifth avenue, new york, n.y. 10016